WHAT IF THE MOON SUDDENLY DISAPPEARS?

AND 20 OTHER 'WHAT IFS' TO BLOW YOUR MIND

ATREYI KAUL

Made with ♥ on the Notion Press Platform
www.notionpress.com

Contents

Contents

WHAT IF THE MOON SUDDENLY DISAPPEARS?

Atreyi Kaul is a curious and creative high school student based in Bengaluru, India, with a deep love for science and storytelling. A top academic performer and a passionate explorer of ideas, she blends imagination with knowledge to craft engaging content for young minds. Her journey into writing began with a fascination for the strange, surprising twists of everyday life and the universe.

You can reach out to her via:

Email: kaulatreyi@gmail.com

LinkedIn: linkedin.com/in/atreyi-kaul

Foreword

Every great discovery begins with a question—a simple, curious spark that sets the mind alight. What if the moon suddenly disappeared? What if gravity stopped working for just a few seconds? These questions might seem like the stuff of daydreams or science fiction, but they are also gateways to understanding the universe in new and surprising ways.

In this book, Atreyi Kaul takes readers on an extraordinary journey through 21 "what if" scenarios that challenge how we think about the world around us. With a blend of scientific insight, imagination, and a genuine love for curiosity, Atreyi invites readers—young and old alike—to explore possibilities that push the boundaries of reality and ignite the imagination.

As a student, innovator, and thinker, Atreyi reminds us that no question is too big or too strange to explore. Her writing is accessible, fun, and thought-provoking, making complex science feel like an adventure rather than a lesson.

Whether you're a budding scientist, a daydreamer, or someone who loves a good mind-bender, this book will inspire you to ask more questions and never stop wondering. Because the world is far more fascinating when we dare to ask, "What if?"

PREFACE

Have you ever looked up at the sky and thought, what if the moon just... disappeared?

I have.

In fact, I think about weird questions like that all the time.

What if we didn't need to sleep? What if gravity stopped working for a few seconds? What if your dreams were actually real in another universe? Crazy, right? But the thing is—behind every one of those "what ifs" lies a whole world of science, imagination, and endless possibilities.

That's exactly what this book is about.

I'm just a student—probably a lot like you. I don't have a spaceship (yet), but I do have questions. Big ones. Weird ones. Fun ones. And instead of just googling them, I decided to dive deep, explore the science, and write down everything I found in a way that doesn't feel like a boring textbook.

This book contains 21 thought-provoking questions. Some are mind-blowingly impossible. Some could actually happen. But all of them will make you think in a way you probably haven't before.

So, if you've ever wondered what would happen if the world worked a little differently, turn the page. Let's question everything—together.

Get ready to blow your own mind. What are you waiting for?

Acknowledgements

Writing this book has been an incredible journey of curiosity and discovery, and I couldn't have done it alone.

A big thanks to my teachers and mentors who nurtured my love for science and helped me turn wild ideas into something meaningful.

And thank you to every curious reader who picks up this book. Your questions and imagination are what truly make this journey worthwhile.

Let's keep wondering, questioning, and exploring—because the world is full of amazing possibilities waiting to be discovered.

— Atreyi Kaul

Prologue

Imagine waking up one morning to find the moon missing from the sky. No glowing orb lighting the night, no tides pulling the oceans, just an empty space where the moon used to be. How would the world change? How would you change?

This question, like many others in this book, isn't just about facts—it's about wondering what if the rules we take for granted suddenly flipped. What if reality played a trick on us?

Each chapter in this book is a doorway to a different "what if" — some strange, some thrilling, some even a little scary. But through every question, there's a chance to think deeper, imagine bigger, and explore how science and creativity come together.

So, before diving into these mind-bending ideas, take a moment to let your imagination run wild. Because sometimes, the most incredible discoveries start with a single question that seems too strange to be true.

Are you ready? The universe is waiting.

I
What If The Moon Suddenly Disappears?

Imagine this: You step outside one evening, ready to admire the full moon. But something's off. You look up — and boom. It's gone. No moon. Just a bunch of confused stars looking around like, "Who turned off the spotlight?"

Did it ghost us? Did it go on vacation to Saturn? Did aliens borrow it for a galaxy-wide moonwalk competition? Or maybe — just maybe — Earth forgot to pay its satellite subscription fee. (Oops.)

Jokes aside, the moon isn't just a beautiful decoration in the sky. It's more like Earth's silent life coach. Always there, not saying much, but making sure everything stays balanced. From keeping our oceans in check to making sure we don't spin like a rogue fidget spinner, the moon plays a massive role in our everyday lives — even if we don't notice it.

So... what would really happen if the moon disappeared overnight?

Spoiler alert: Things would get weird. And a little scary. But mostly... weird.

1. Tides Would Have a Meltdown (Literally)

First things first — the tides.

Right now, the moon acts like a cosmic magnet, pulling on Earth's oceans and making the water rise and fall in a beautiful, reliable rhythm. That's what creates tides — the gentle ebb and flow that surfers love, fishermen depend on, and beachside *chaiwalas* time their snack breaks around.

But here's the science: the moon is responsible for around 70–75% of Earth's tidal activity. The rest comes from the sun, but its gravitational effect on Earth's water is only about 46% as strong as the moon's. So, if the moon disappeared, you could say goodbye to high tides as we know them.

Instead of the regular highs and lows, tides would become weaker and unpredictable. And this wouldn't just mess up your beach day — it would mess up the whole ocean.

You see, marine life is closely linked to the tides. Take mussels, barnacles, and starfish — they rely on the tidal rhythm for feeding, breeding, and even breathing. Coral reefs, which house more than 25% of marine species, could suffer huge setbacks in reproduction because many coral species spawn based on lunar cycles. No moon = no timing.

And what about nutrient mixing in oceans? Tides play a major role in moving nutrients from the deep sea to the surface. This helps plankton grow — and plankton is the foundation of the ocean food chain. Disrupt that, and the entire system can collapse.

Also, without strong tides, coastal erosion patterns would shift. Some beaches might shrink; others might grow. Estuaries and deltas, like the Sundarbans in India, would change shape. Fishing industries could suffer, too.

In short, no moon = confused oceans = struggling ecosystems.

2. Earth Would Start Spinning Faster (Like It's in a Hurry)

Let's talk about Earth's rotation. Right now, we have nice 24-hour days — just long enough to sleep, study, eat, panic over exams, scroll through reels, and repeat.

But here's something wild: the moon is slowly making Earth spin slower. It's called "tidal braking." As the moon's gravity pulls on Earth, it causes friction that slows our spin. Without it, Earth would start to speed up.

If the moon suddenly vanished, Earth's days could gradually shorten to 18 hours — or even less over millions of years. That means you'd have only 6 hours of sleep, 5 hours of school, and probably 7 hours of trying to do all your homework while also binge-watching your favorite show.

But wait, it gets worse.

Earth doesn't just spin — it tilts. And that tilt (about 23.5°) is what gives us seasons. Spring, summer, autumn, and winter — all because Earth is slightly off-kilter. The moon acts like a stabilizing anchor, keeping that tilt from going haywire. Without it, Earth's axial tilt could start wobbling between 0° and 45°, and possibly even up to 90°. That means some parts of the planet could end up with 6 months of total sunlight, followed by 6 months of complete darkness — similar to what happens near the poles, but even more extreme. That's not just creepy — it's dangerous.

If the tilt shifts too much, climate zones would flip. Deserts could become rainforests. Tropical zones could freeze. Crops would fail. Food supplies would be messed up. Wildlife migration patterns would be destroyed. And humans? We'd either have to move, adapt, or invent climate-controlling technology fast.

So yes — the moon is keeping us from turning into a frozen hot mess.

3. Earth's Weather Patterns Would Freak Out

Now let's talk about the weather. If the moon's gone, the tides weaken, Earth spins faster, and the tilt goes bananas — what do you think happens to the weather?

Exactly. Chaos.

Weather patterns depend on consistent rotation and solar energy. If days shorten, heat from the sun won't be distributed properly. Fast spinning could create stronger jet streams and mega-storms. The wobbling tilt would make seasons unpredictable. Imagine having a snowstorm in the middle of what used to be summer.

And remember how the moon helps mix the ocean water? That also helps regulate Earth's temperature. Without that, we could see overheating in some areas and extreme cooling in others. Basically, weather would stop being your friendly neighborhood climate and turn into an unpredictable beast.

Floods, droughts, mega hurricanes — all could become more common. And not just for a few years. This would be Earth's new normal.

4. Wildlife Would Lose Their Natural Clock

This one's a bit sad.

Animals — especially nocturnal and coastal ones — use the moon like a natural clock. From sea turtles to coral to wolves to birds, many species depend on moonlight or lunar cycles to guide their behavior.

For example:

Sea turtles lay eggs based on the lunar calendar. Without it, they might lay them at the wrong time, reducing baby survival rates.

Corals in places like the Great Barrier Reef reproduce all at once during specific moon phases. Without the moon's cue, they'd become unsynchronized, and reefs could collapse.

Birds use the moon and stars to navigate during migration. Without the moon, they'd get lost.

Nocturnal animals like owls or foxes hunt better with moonlight. If it's gone, their hunting patterns would change, affecting their survival and the balance of prey and predators.

Even some insects time their life cycles with the moon. Fireflies, frogs, moths — all follow lunar cues.

And here's a strange one: human behavior might also be affected. Some studies show that sleep cycles and even moods are subtly influenced by the moon's presence. No moon could mean more irregular sleep, anxiety, or mood swings.

So yeah. If the moon disappears, it's not just the animals that get confused. We might feel a little off, too.

5. No More Moonlight — and That's a Problem

Moonlight isn't just beautiful. It plays a real role in life on Earth.

The moon reflects sunlight, and that light helps animals move at night. It also helps plants like night-blooming jasmine and moonflowers, which rely on moonlight to trigger their bloom.

Without it, nights would be darker — especially in rural or wild areas. That might sound cosy, but it's not great for nocturnal navigation. Imagine you're a wild deer and suddenly the only streetlights you had — moonbeams — vanish. Oof.

And remember those beautiful lunar eclipses and moon-viewing festivals? Gone. So would poems about the moon. (Sorry, Shakespeare.)

6. The Moon's Disappearance Would Mess With Gravity — Slightly

Here's another brain-bender: the moon actually affects Earth's shape.

Because the moon pulls on Earth, it causes what scientists call "Earth tides" — not just in water, but in the crust itself! Earth's solid surface rises and falls by about 30 centimeters each day due to the moon's gravity.

Take the moon away, and the balance of forces changes. Earth might slightly shift shape — not enough to be dramatic, but enough to affect seismic activity. That's right: more earthquakes and possibly volcanic eruptions could result from the sudden rebalancing of forces.

It's like pulling one leg of a table away — everything shakes, even if only a little.

7. Space Might Become a Lot Lonelier (And More Dangerous)

The moon has always been part of human dreams. It's the first celestial body humans stepped on. It helps block some meteors that might otherwise crash into us. It even protects Earth from some space debris.

If it were gone, Earth would be a slightly bigger target. That doesn't mean we'd suddenly get bombarded with meteorites, but we'd lose a bit of protection — kind of like taking the goalie out of a football match.

Also, without the moon, our understanding of space would take a hit. Astronomers use the moon as a reference point. Future moon bases, lunar telescopes, or mining missions? Gone.

So... Could This Actually Happen?

Nope. At least not naturally.

The moon is slowly moving away from Earth at a rate of about 3.8 centimeters per year. But don't panic — it'll take billions of years for it to drift too far to affect us. So unless aliens really want a souvenir, the moon isn't disappearing any time soon.

Final Thoughts: The Moon Is More Than Just a Pretty Face

It controls tides. It balances our tilt. It keeps Earth spinning smoothly. It guides animals, affects our sleep, and lights up the night. Take it away, and Earth becomes... well, a little bit broken.

So next time you see the moon — whether it's a full glowing circle or just a crescent banana in the sky — give it a silent thank-you.

It's not just Earth's satellite. It's our planet's unsung hero.

II

What If Humans Could Photosynthesize?

Before we dive into this leafy, green idea, let's take a little stroll through photosynthesis history class. Don't worry — I'll keep it fun, no pop quizzes!

The Magic Behind Photosynthesis — A Quick Refresher

Remember back in school, when your teachers made you memorise terms like chloroplasts, stomata, and glucose? Maybe you asked yourself, Why do I even need to know this?

Spoiler: It's actually super important. Photosynthesis isn't just some boring biology lesson—it's the life engine for almost everything on Earth.

Here's the deal: photosynthesis is the amazing process by which plants, algae, and some bacteria capture sunlight and turn it into food — and oxygen, which is what we breathe.

In fancy science words:

Photosynthesis is a biological process that converts light energy into chemical energy, stored as glucose molecules, using water and carbon dioxide

But let's break it down into human-friendly language:

Photo means "light." Synthesis means "to put together."

So, photosynthesis means "putting things together using light." Plants take sunlight, mix it with water from their roots and carbon dioxide from the air, and make sugar (food) and oxygen (which they kindly give us). That's why leaves are green — because of a pigment called chlorophyll, which acts like a solar panel inside every leaf. Thanks to photosynthesis, plants not only feed themselves but also feed us indirectly, and keep our atmosphere filled with oxygen. In fact, without photosynthesis, Earth would be a very different place — no plants, no animals, and definitely no humans.

So What If Humans Could Photosynthesize?

Sounds like a fun sci-fi idea, right? Imagine a world where humans don't have to worry about lunch, dinner, or midnight snacks. Just walk outside, catch some rays, and boom — instant energy, just like a plant. You might picture people sunbathing in parks like giant green leaves, arms spread wide, basking in the sunlight.

But here's the kicker — for humans to photosynthesize, our bodies would have to undergo some mind-blowing transformations. Let's explore what would need to happen.

1. Humans Would Need Chloroplasts — The Green Factories

Chloroplasts are tiny structures inside plant cells where all photosynthesis happens. For humans to photosynthesize, our cells would somehow have to develop chloroplasts or something similar.

Sounds cool, but there's a problem: human cells aren't designed for this. Plants have specialized cells with cell walls, chloroplasts, and huge surface areas (like leaves) optimized to capture sunlight. Our skin cells don't have chloroplasts, nor can they suddenly grow them.

Scientists have actually experimented with putting chloroplasts or algae into animal cells, but it's extremely complicated. Chloroplasts need tons of support systems and constant care from the cell, and animal cells aren't built for that.

So for us to truly photosynthesize, evolution or genetic engineering would have to rewrite our biology completely.

2. Green-Tinted Skin — Sorry, No More Pale or Tan

If our bodies produced chlorophyll, we'd have green skin — or at least some shade of green. So say goodbye to your usual skin tone; you'd be rocking the chlorophyll look all day, every day.

That would definitely change the whole skincare industry. No more sunscreen? Or maybe we'd invent "chlorophyll-friendly" sunblock. Green would be the new black.

On the bright side, maybe Halloween costumes would become easier — just roll out in your natural green!

3. More Surface Area — Arms Like Leaves?

Photosynthesis requires sunlight exposure, so humans would likely need to increase their skin's surface area to absorb enough light. Maybe our arms would grow wider and flatter, or we'd develop leaf-like extensions. Imagine kids playing "leaf tag" instead of normal tag!

Sounds funny, but having extra skin surface would mean more exposure to the sun — and also more vulnerability to sunburn and environmental damage. On the upside, we'd get our daily dose of vitamin D while photosynthesizing.

4. Still Need Food — But Less of It

Here's where the myth-busting starts.

Photosynthesis can make glucose, which provides energy, but that doesn't give us everything we need. Humans require a range of nutrients: proteins, fats, vitamins, minerals, amino acids, and more. Photosynthesis doesn't supply those.

So even if we could photosynthesize, we'd still need to eat real food. Maybe not three full meals a day, but snacks and nutrient-rich foods would still be essential.

That means pizza nights and birthday cakes would stay in business. Sorry, vegans and raw-foodists — photosynthesis doesn't replace your dinner party just yet.

5. The Sunlight Problem — Long Hours Needed for Energy

Plants are pros at photosynthesis — but they're stationary and have all day to soak in sunlight. Humans? We move around, wear clothes, and often spend time indoors or in shade. Studies show that a single leaf under full sun for 6-8 hours can produce the equivalent energy of a few calories — about what you'd get from a leaf of lettuce. That's not enough to power a whole human body's energy needs.

For humans to get a significant energy boost from photosynthesis, we'd need to spend most of our day outside in direct sunlight with large parts of our skin exposed.

Think of the implications:

Indoor jobs might become impossible without special "sun lamps."

Wearing clothes might have to change — hello, minimalistic fashion!

Cloudy or rainy days would leave us feeling hungry and tired.

So photosynthesis might make us energy-efficient, but only if we're professional sunbathers.

6. Gas Exchange Pores — Would We Need Stomata?

Plants breathe through tiny pores called stomata that open and close to exchange gases — taking in carbon dioxide and releasing oxygen.

If humans photosynthesized, would we develop stomata-like pores in our skin? Maybe. But pores in skin also mean vulnerability to infection, dehydration, and pollution.

Imagine tiny holes all over your skin opening and closing as you breathe carbon dioxide — sounds a bit risky, right?

The evolutionary trade-off would be enormous. We'd need new immune defences, new skin care routines, and a lot of hydration.

7. *Vulnerability to Environment — Weather, Pollution, and Shade*

Photosynthesis depends on light, water, and carbon dioxide — which means photosynthetic humans would be vulnerable to:

Weather: Cloudy days, rain, or cold weather would limit energy production. No sun, no photosynthesis. That might lead to "photosynthesis fatigue" or energy crashes.

Pollution: Smog and air pollution reduce sunlight and damage skin. So urban areas might be a no-go zone for photosynthetic humans.

Shade: Trees, buildings, or clothing blocking the sun would make us hungry.

It's a fragile lifestyle.

8. *What About Night? And What About Winter?*

Humans need energy 24/7, but photosynthesis only happens with light.

So at night — and during long winters in polar regions — photosynthesis would shut down completely. That means relying on stored food or traditional eating at night.

Also, what about caves, basements, or underground spaces? Without sunlight, no photosynthesis. That's a major limitation for modern humans who spend so much time indoors.

9. *Would We Need to Change Our Behaviour and Lifestyle?*

If photosynthesis became a key source of energy, human lifestyles would change drastically:

Outdoor activities would dominate daily routines.

Work schedules might shift to daylight hours only.

Clothes would be designed for maximum sun exposure and protection from UV damage.

Diets might focus more on nutrients we can't get from photosynthesis (like proteins and fats).

Social life might revolve around sunny days and outdoor gatherings.

Basically, humans would start living a lot more like plants — rooted to the sun.

10. *Could Photosynthesis Affect Human Intelligence or Evolution?*

Here's a crazy thought: photosynthesis is efficient but slow. Would relying on photosynthesis affect brain function? Our brains use a lot of energy — about 20% of the body's total energy.

If photosynthesis provides less energy compared to eating food, could it limit cognitive abilities? Would humans have to evolve bigger brains and smaller bodies, or slower metabolism? Would creativity and problem-solving suffer?

On the flip side, perhaps photosynthetic humans might develop symbiotic relationships with other organisms, similar to coral and algae. This could open new paths in evolution.

11. *Environmental Impact — Would Photosynthetic Humans Be Good for the Planet?*

Let's look at the bigger picture.

If humans needed less food because they photosynthesized, the pressure on farming, livestock, and deforestation could decrease. Less farming means less water use, fewer greenhouse gases, and less habitat destruction.

Sounds awesome, right?

But increased sun exposure could lead to higher water loss from skin (transpiration-like effects), possibly increasing human water needs.

Plus, the sudden evolution or genetic engineering of photosynthetic humans could have unpredictable ecological impacts.

12. *Could Science Make This Happen?*

Could humans be genetically engineered to photosynthesize?

Scientists are exploring ways to transfer photosynthetic abilities to animals or human cells. For example:

Some research shows algae inserted into animal cells can survive temporarily.

Attempts to engineer photosynthetic skin bacteria to boost energy.

Synthetic biology might one day create hybrid cells.

But these are early-stage, highly complex projects with many ethical, medical, and practical challenges.

So... Should We Want to Photosynthesize?

Let's weigh the pros and cons:
Pros:
Reduced need for food and farming.
Sustainable energy source from sunlight.
Possible lower carbon footprint.
Close connection with nature.
Cons:
Slow energy production — would need constant sun.
Big biological changes, including green skin and new anatomy.
Vulnerability to weather, pollution, and night.
Still need to eat other nutrients.
Social and cultural changes — no more hiding under clothes, no midnight snacks!

Final Thoughts — Let's Leave Photosynthesis to the Plants

As wild as it sounds, human photosynthesis is a fascinating thought experiment but probably not practical for us. We love food way too much — the taste, the culture, the joy of sharing meals. Maybe it's best to admire plants for their amazing skills and thank them quietly every time we take a breath. After all, they've been doing the photosynthesis thing just fine for hundreds of millions of years — and we're pretty good at cooking and ordering food.

But Hey — It's Fun to Imagine!

This is exactly what science and imagination are for: to ask crazy questions, explore wild ideas, and laugh at how bizarre the universe can be.

So next time you're out in the sun, think about what it'd be like if you could just stand there, arms outstretched, soaking up energy — a walking, talking, photosynthetic marvel.

And if you suddenly start turning green... well, maybe it's time to see a doctor. Or a botanist.

If you liked this green adventure, wait till you hear about humans with wings, or what if we could breathe underwater!

Stay curious, keep imagining, and don't forget your sunscreen.

III

What If Gravity Suddenly Switched Off For 10 Seconds?

Okay, hear me out.

You're walking to school with your backpack full of books, lunchbox swinging at your side, and suddenly—whoosh!—your feet lift off the ground. Your sandwich is doing somersaults in mid-air. The kid next to you is flailing like he's on an invisible rollercoaster. And somewhere in the distance, an unfortunate cat floats by with a very confused look on its face.

No, this isn't the trailer for some new superhero movie. This is what could happen if gravity just... stopped working. Poof. Gone. For 10 full seconds.

Sounds fun, right?

Well, not exactly. Let's dig a little deeper—and maybe hold on to something sturdy while we're at it.

Gravity: The Invisible Glue

Gravity is the force that pulls everything towards everything else. On Earth, it's what keeps you from floating off into the sky like an untethered balloon. It's why waterfalls fall down, why your glass of water stays in the glass, and why you don't lose your chapati to the ceiling every time you have lunch.

Long before we had space agencies and satellites, ancient Indian thinkers like Aryabhata and later Bhaskaracharya were already pondering over why objects fall toward the Earth. In his 12th-century text Siddhanta Shiromani, Bhaskaracharya wrote about "gurutva karshan," which means the Earth attracts objects towards itself. It wasn't called "gravity" yet, but the idea was spot on.

Fast forward to the 17th century, and Sir Isaac Newton gave us the classical explanation: gravity is the force of attraction between two masses. His famous story of an apple falling from a tree sparked centuries of science (whether or not he actually got hit on the head is up for debate). Newton's law of universal gravitation says that everything with mass pulls on everything else with a force that depends on their masses and the distance between them.

And then came Einstein with his General Theory of Relativity, showing us that gravity isn't just a force but a bending of space and time itself. Picture the Earth as a heavy ball on a stretched rubber sheet, warping the sheet and causing smaller objects to roll towards it. Mind-bending stuff, literally!

Now imagine that this gurutva karshan decided to take a 10-second coffee break.

Get Ready — 10 Seconds Before Total Floating Chaos Begins!

If gravity switched off, everything not anchored (and even some things that are) would start to float. You, your desk, your neighbor's scooter, the water in your fish tank, the actual fish in your fish tank... all slowly lifting off like there's a magician in the sky pulling a prank.

Cars would become confused hovercrafts. Birds would flap helplessly in all directions. Planes? Let's just say the passengers would be clinging to their seatbelts for dear life—or maybe to the floating samosas from the in-flight meal.

Even the air around us would start drifting away, which means breathing could get tricky pretty fast.

Will We Fly Into Space?

Thankfully, no — we're not about to turn into accidental astronauts.

While gravity is what keeps us anchored to the Earth, turning it off for 10 seconds wouldn't launch us into deep space like a rocket. Why? Because escaping Earth's gravity permanently requires escape velocity, which is about 11.2 kilometers per second (roughly 40,000 km/h). In comparison, the sudden loss of gravity wouldn't give us nearly that kind of speed.

But here's where it gets interesting: Earth is constantly rotating, spinning around its axis at approximately 1,670 kilometers per hour at the equator. Normally, gravity counters the outward pull this spin creates. But if gravity were to suddenly vanish, that balancing force disappears—and now, we're at the mercy of Earth's motion.

So instead of floating gently straight up, objects (and people) would start to drift sideways—sort of like when you let go of something in a spinning car. That drift would depend on your location and momentum.

Closer to the equator, the sideways motion would be stronger because the rotational speed is greatest there. Near the poles, it would be far less noticeable.

You wouldn't gain enough velocity to break through Earth's atmosphere, but you could easily float a few meters—or even tens of meters—away from your original position.

Picture this: you're standing in your garden, and suddenly you're airborne, gliding slightly sideways, only to land a few houses down once gravity returns. If you're unlucky, you might land on someone's rooftop, or worse—get tangled in electric wires, trees, or (classic cartoon style) a clothesline with someone's bedsheets on it.

Air and Atmosphere on the Loose

Another factor is air resistance. As the atmosphere itself is made of particles affected by gravity, those particles would start to move too. That means air would no longer press down on you as it usually does, and you'd be moving through a thinning, shifting atmosphere.

Breathing would become harder, and objects wouldn't slow down as they normally do when moving through air. Imagine trying to blow out birthday candles, but the air around you is floating away, and the usual "whoosh" sound is missing. Weird, right?

What About Oceans, Rivers, and Lakes?

Think bigger now

Oceans, lakes, rivers — all held to Earth's surface by gravity. What happens when gravity drops out for 10 seconds? Water would start to float. Not just a little splash, but entire huge volumes of water breaking free from their beds, rising into the air in massive floating blobs. It would be a watery chaos: sudden floating puddles, droplets, and even fish suspended mid-air, flapping their fins like confused swimmers in zero gravity.

When gravity snaps back, all that water would come crashing down with the force of hundreds of waterfalls landing at once, causing massive flooding and destruction in coastal and riverside areas.

Human Physiology in Zero Gravity for 10 Seconds

Even 10 seconds in zero gravity would wreak havoc on our bodies.

Our muscles and bones are used to working against gravity constantly. Astronauts who stay in space for months lose bone density and muscle mass because they don't have to fight gravity's pull.

Now, while 10 seconds isn't enough to cause long-term damage, the sudden float and crash could cause serious injuries: bumps, bruises, broken bones from falls or flying objects. Your blood would temporarily redistribute. Normally, gravity pulls blood toward your feet, but without it, blood shifts toward your head, which might give you a brief feeling of head rush or pressure.

Balance would go haywire. Your inner ear relies on gravity to tell which way is up. Without it, people might feel dizzy or disoriented.

What Happens to Birds, Planes, and Flying Things?

Birds would be in total confusion. Their entire flight depends on gravity and air resistance to control movement and landing.

Imagine pigeons, sparrows, or even eagles suddenly floating without control, flapping frantically, bumping into each other or getting caught in floating debris.

Planes mid-flight would be a nightmare. Passengers would experience sudden weightlessness, then a crash landing effect. Pilots would struggle to control planes with no gravitational pull, and unsecured items inside cabins would fly everywhere.

Space Stations and Satellites

While gravity on Earth would vanish, satellites and space stations already orbit Earth in a state of microgravity. But the gravity from Earth still holds them in orbit.

If Earth's gravity switched off completely for 10 seconds, satellites might drift slightly off course, potentially disrupting communications and GPS signals.

Though this might be minor in 10 seconds, repeated gravity failures could throw satellites out of orbit entirely, causing them to fall back to Earth or drift off into space.

The Return of Gravity — And the Fallout

After 10 seconds of blissful, chaotic floatation, gravity flips the switch and suddenly snaps back into action—no warning, no gentle transition, no cinematic countdown.

And then... everything crashes down.

What was a peaceful (and slightly hilarious) zero-gravity moment instantly becomes a global catastrophe. Remember, during those 10 seconds, everything was not just floating, but also moving—carried by Earth's spin, by their own momentum, or even by slight gusts of air.

So when gravity returns, it doesn't gently guide objects back to the ground—it yanks them straight down, wherever they are. Think of it as a planet-wide, high-speed game of dodgeball, except the balls are refrigerators, flower pots, smartphones, ceiling fans, motorbikes, and unfortunately... humans.

People who were inside elevators? They'll find themselves in a sudden freefall the moment gravity comes back. Elevators might jolt or crash, depending on safety systems.

Kids jumping on trampolines or people in the middle of a basketball dunk? Smacked to the ground.

Birds, drones, and kites? Dive-bombing like meteorites.

Water? It was floating too. Now it turns into sudden, localized downpours, slamming into the ground, streets, and unsuspecting people like gravity-powered water balloons.

Airplanes at high altitudes? Passengers would experience a terrifying drop inside the cabin. And anything not strapped in—like food trays or the occasional laptop—would become high-speed projectiles.

Even worse: things that drifted sideways due to Earth's rotation are now falling off-center—smashing into trees, crashing through roofs, and breaking a few unfortunate windshields on the way. An open toolbox might rain down hammers and spanners like a hardware store apocalypse.

Meanwhile, inside homes and buildings:

Ceiling fans may have wobbled loose and now drop straight onto tables.

Books fly back to shelves—and miss.

Your lunchbox? Exploded on the kitchen floor.

Your sandwich? It might have reached escape velocity from your hand during the float, and now returns like a soggy, mustard-smeared boomerang. Target: your face.

Hospitals would overflow with injuries. Emergency services would be in panic mode. People would be dazed, bruised, and incredibly confused.

And scientists? They'd be speechless—for about 30 seconds, before launching a global investigation and rewriting entire physics textbooks.

What Does This Mean for Science?

Gravity is one of the four fundamental forces of nature—alongside electromagnetism, the weak nuclear force, and the strong nuclear force. These forces are the invisible threads that weave together the entire universe. Gravity, in particular, is the quiet, persistent one—subtle compared to the explosive power of nuclear forces, but absolutely essential. It shapes planets, orchestrates the motion of stars, binds galaxies, and anchors you to the Earth every moment of your life.

If gravity could switch off—even for just 10 seconds—it suggests something astonishing: that there's a deeper mechanism at work, something we haven't yet grasped. Maybe there's a hidden layer of physics we haven't uncovered, or an interdimensional switchboard pulling the strings from behind the cosmic curtain. Could gravity be a "tunable" force, something we could one day control or modify like temperature or electricity?

If so, we'd have to rethink physics entirely.

The textbooks would be toast. Space travel, weather systems, ocean currents, tectonic plates, tides, tree growth, and even the way your heart pumps blood—they all depend on gravity in one way or another. Turning it off would unravel nearly every natural process we understand.

But now flip that thought: what if we could manipulate gravity at will?

No more need for fossil-fueled transportation. Cars could float. Cities could hover. Heavy machinery could become weightless during construction, making skyscrapers as easy to build as LEGO towers. Medical procedures could be transformed. Sports would become three-dimensional. We could live on asteroids, colonize the Moon with ease, or send ships into space without the energy costs of rocket launches.

Sounds incredible—until you realize the dangers.

Weapons that remove gravity from specific zones. Prisons floating in space. Machines that could crush or launch anything with the flick of a dial. A single gravity failure in a city could cause buildings to crumble and people to rise like bubbles in soda, only to crash down seconds later.

In the right hands, controlled gravity could be the next leap of civilization.

In the wrong ones? It could be the undoing of everything.

Either way, one thing becomes clear: gravity isn't just some invisible force that keeps your cereal from floating out of your bowl. It's a gateway—a frontier. And if it can flicker, pause, or bend, it means our understanding of the universe is just getting started.

So Next Time You Complain About Your Heavy Backpack...

Take a moment to appreciate gravity.

Because without it, Earth becomes a chaos simulator—and you're stuck in the middle of it, probably dodging toasters, tumbling furniture, and airborne gadgets doing somersaults in midair. That heavy backpack? It might be annoying when you're trudging uphill to school, but it's the reason you're not bouncing off the stratosphere or getting launched into the ceiling like a human rocket.

Gravity might seem like a boring background force, always pulling, always present, always slowing us down. But it's also the reason your feet stay on the ground, your cereal stays in the bowl, your oceans stay on the planet, and the Moon doesn't decide to pack up and drift away. That's the same force keeping the planets in orbit, steering comets, and sculpting galaxies.

So yeah, your backpack is heavy. But you know what's heavier? The idea of a world without gravity — a world where water won't pour, where fires won't burn, where your bones weaken, and your sense of direction floats away with your lunchbox. In that world, even a single sip of water becomes a puzzle. A walk down the hall becomes a gymnastics routine. And a nap? You'd better strap yourself to the bed unless you want to wake up on the ceiling.

The next time you feel like complaining about how gravity is dragging you down — literally — remember that it's also holding everything together. You, your home, your family, your entire world.

Without gravity, it's not just your backpack that goes flying. It's life itself that loses its grip. So, lift that bag with pride.

Because, thanks to gravity, at least you know where "down" is.

IV

What If The Earth Stopped Rotating?

Stopped rotating? Fine. Anyways, we aren't rotating with the Earth, are we? It surely wouldn't impact us, right?

NO.

Wrong.

It's unthinkable to imagine what would happen if the Earth actually stopped rotating. Scary, right? Imagine you're peacefully eating a slice of pizza and suddenly — BOOM — the Earth slams the brakes like it saw a speed bump the size of Jupiter. Chaos would follow. Let's get into some conceptualities, facts, and yes, even a little doom (with some jokes to keep your existential dread at bay).

First, Let's Understand What Rotation Even Does

The Earth rotates at about 1,670 kilometers per hour (1,038 mph) at the equator. That's faster than most jet planes. This rotation is what causes day and night, influences weather patterns, and even helps create Earth's shape — slightly squished at the poles and bulging at the equator.

Now, if the Earth were to suddenly stop rotating — not gradually slow down, but screech to a halt — we'd be in BIG trouble. Like, "I left the stove on" levels of trouble, but for the whole planet.

Let's imagine the different consequences...

1. INERTIA: The Planet-Wide Slingshot

According to Newton's First Law of Motion, an object in motion stays in motion unless acted upon by an external force. That means everything not firmly attached to the Earth — oceans, air, buildings, people, your cat, your fridge — would keep moving at 1,670 km/h (that's faster than a bullet, by the way).

So what happens?

Everything gets launched eastward.

Mountains? Flattened.

Cities? Scraped off the surface like toppings off a badly-thrown pizza.

You? Turned into human spaghetti in mid-air.

It would feel like being in a car crash... but with the entire Earth. Instant mass destruction.

"QUICK LOOK INTO INERTIA

Inertia is an object's resistance to change in its motion. If something is still, it wants to stay still. If it's moving, it wants to keep moving — unless something forces it to stop or change direction. So, when Earth spins at about 1,670 km/h (1,038 mph) at the equator, we're all moving with it. If Earth suddenly stopped spinning...Our inertia would keep us flying forward at that same speed — like coffee spilling forward in a car that hits the brakes too hard. Only in this case, you are the coffee. "

2. MEGA TSUNAMIS: *Surf's Up... Forever*

Let's talk about oceans. Water isn't anchored to the Earth's crust. So when the Earth stops, the oceans will keep moving, forming waves that are hundreds, even thousands, of meters high.

These super tsunamis would travel across continents, drowning coastlines, sweeping inland for hundreds of kilometers. Goodbye Miami. Sayonara Singapore. Adios Mumbai.

Even continents could erode away in some regions. Earth's coastlines would be redrawn like a toddler doodling with crayons on a world map.

3. HURRICANIC HYSTERIA: *Atmospheric Havoc*

Now imagine what happens to the air. Earth's rotation influences wind patterns through something called the Coriolis effect. It's what helps create trade winds, cyclones, and jet streams.

No rotation = no Coriolis effect = the entire atmosphere goes bananas.

Massive supersonic winds would race across the surface. Cities already flattened by tsunamis would get sandblasted by dust storms. It's like Earth turned into a blender, and we're all the ingredients. Also, the weather system as we know it would collapse. Say goodbye to seasons, storms, and that awkward "it's too hot for jeans but too cold for shorts" weather.

4. NO MORE 24-HOUR DAYS

If Earth stops rotating but continues to orbit the Sun (which is possible in theory), then each side of the planet would get 6 months of daylight and 6 months of night.

Sounds cool? Think again.

6 months of sunlight = unbearable heat. Crops die. Rivers evaporate. Skin sizzles like bacon.

6 months of darkness = freezing cold.

Polar temperatures all over. Plants can't photosynthesize. Food becomes rarer than a unicorn on a skateboard. This is bad news.

5. THE SHAPE OF THE EARTH WILL CHANGE

Because of Earth's rotation, it's not a perfect sphere — it bulges at the equator. If the rotation stops, gravity will redistribute itself more evenly. The Earth would become more spherical.

That means:

Water near the equator would flow toward the poles. The equator would become landlocked. New oceans would form around the poles. Sea levels in currently equatorial countries would drop dramatically, leaving cities stranded inland.

So, if you own beachfront property — too bad, it's now desert real estate.

6. SAY GOODBYE TO EARTH'S MAGNETIC FIELD

Earth's magnetic field is generated by the motion of molten iron in its outer core — a movement influenced by rotation. If Earth stops rotating, that dynamo effect could fade or vanish completely. The result?

No magnetic field. No protection from solar radiation. Frequent blackouts from solar storms. Radiation exposure = higher cancer risk + fried satellites.

Basically, without the magnetic field, we'd be like an egg frying on a cosmic pan, constantly bombarded by solar particles.

7. WALKING WOULD BE... DIFFERENT?

Here's a weird one. Because of centrifugal force due to Earth's spin, objects weigh slightly less at the equator than at the poles.

If rotation stops? You'll weigh more. At the equator, you'd gain roughly 0.3% more weight. Not much, but enough to make your weighing scale a little ruder in the morning.

So no, your sudden weight gain is not because of cookies. It's because Earth decided to take a nap.

8. GLOBAL GEOPOLITICS = MADNESS

Imagine governments trying to deal with:
One side of the world baking under the sun.
Another in complete darkness.
Food and water shortages.
Mass migrations.

Collapsing economies.

It's a global crisis of apocalyptic proportions. The United Nations would need a miracle (and maybe Iron Man) to hold things together.

Fun fact: In some simulations, it's theorized that the equator region would become uninhabitable while the "twilight zone" — the areas between permanent night and day — would become the new prime real estate.

9. OKAY, WHAT IF IT STOPPED SLOWLY?

Ah, the peaceful version! What if Earth gradually slowed over millions of years?

That's more realistic and less apocalyptic.

Here's what might happen:

Days would slowly lengthen — imagine a 40-hour day! More Netflix, right?

Life would adapt: Plants could photosynthesize longer; humans might evolve new sleep patterns.

Magnetic field might still weaken over time.

Climate zones would shift.

Equatorial bulge would shrink, slowly changing sea levels.

This scenario is way less "fiery doom" and more "slow-motion sci-fi movie."

10. COULD WE SURVIVE?

Okay, now that's the real question, isn't it?

Let's say Earth stopped rotating but we prepared in advance. Could humanity survive? Technically, yes — but it would take an absurd amount of planning.

We'd need:

Underground cities with stable temperature controls.
Artificial lighting for agriculture.
Massive energy systems to simulate day-night cycles.
A planetary agreement to maintain order and resources.

So yeah, it's possible. But it would require the kind of global cooperation we can't even achieve when deciding what pizza toppings to order.

Let's Do Some Science-y Math

Kinetic Energy of Earth's Rotation:

Earth's rotational kinetic energy is approximately 2.14×1029 joules. That's about a billion times more energy than all nuclear weapons on Earth combined.

Stopping that instantly? Impossible without some kind of space wizardry or a cosmic emergency brake.

Also, if something did have the power to stop the Earth, we'd probably have bigger problems — like the entity that just flexed hard enough to freeze a planet.

Earth's Midlife Crisis?

Let's say Earth just... got tired.

"I've been spinning for 4.5 billion years. I'm done."
sips cosmic coffee
hits pause button
Honestly? Can't blame it.

Maybe it's Earth's version of a midlife crisis. It just decides to stop spinning. Because why not?

Other Planets Have Weird Rotation Too!

Did you know?

Venus rotates so slowly that a day on Venus is longer than its year.

Uranus rotates sideways — like it's permanently sunbathing.

Mercury has no tilt — zero seasons, zero drama.

So yes, planets have weird behaviors. But Earth is special — its rotation helps maintain life as we know it. Remove that rotation, and you remove balance. Earth isn't just spinning for fun. It's spinning for us.

Final Thoughts: Be Glad We're Spinning!

Next time you're bored in science class, staring out the window, or groaning because your alarm clock ruined a perfectly good dream, pause for a second. Remind yourself:

You're standing on a massive, molten-cored, magnetically shielded rock, spinning at over 1,000 miles per hour, dancing gracefully around a star that's 93 million miles away — all without you even feeling it. No roller coaster, no simulator, no theme park ride can compete with the mind-blowing ride you're already on, every single second of your life.

This rotation doesn't just give us day and night. It gives us balance, predictability, and the chance to plan birthdays, write poetry, grow apples, and, well... sleep in sometimes.

If the Earth ever stopped rotating, we wouldn't just lose our sunsets and sunrises — we'd lose everything familiar: our rhythm, our cycles, the patterns we've evolved with for millions of years. In a way, the Earth's spin is like a cosmic lullaby — always there, always humming in the background.

We take it for granted because it's constant. But that's the beauty of it.

So, until the stars stop shining, or some mischievous alien presses the planetary pause button, let's be thankful Earth is still doing its thing — spinning tirelessly, keeping time, keeping life in motion.

And we?

We'll keep spinning with it — hopefully right side up, with our feet on the ground and our heads full of wonder.

So go ahead. Look up.

Smile at the sky. And say,

"Thanks for the spin, Earth. Keep it up."

V

What If You Could Pause Time - But Only For Yourself?

Seems interesting, right? That devil inside you might be racing its thoughts to the wonderous things you could do, if time stopped – only and only for you. But things aren't always the way they look, are they? There's got to be a twist, because not all stories end as expected.

The Fantasy

Okay, picture this: It's Monday morning. Your alarm goes off at 6:00 AM, your math homework is unfinished, your room looks like a tornado just tried origami, and you have a surprise test in physics. Now, what if — just what if — you could pause time?

You lazily lift your hand, snap your fingers (because of course, all cool time-pause moments require a snap), and boom. The world around you freezes. Birds are stuck mid-flight, your dog's drool is floating in mid-air, and your sister's annoying voice? Gloriously muted

You're now walking in a completely still world, a ruler of paused time. You finish homework, clean your room, microwave some noodles, and even practice your evil laugh in front of a mirror. Life's good.

Right?

Eh... maybe not.

The Reality: Let's Break It Down

Let's start with a BIG question: What does it really mean to pause time "for yourself"?

Most people imagine time pausing like hitting the freeze button on a video—everything halts: falling raindrops hang mid-air, people are frozen mid-blink, birds pause mid-flap. And you? You can stroll around, poke the frozen raindrops, maybe even steal someone's pizza without them noticing. Pretty cool, right?

But here's the catch: Physics, as usual, is the annoying friend who ruins movie plots by asking too many questions.

What is time, anyway?

Let's get a little nerdy.

Time, in physics, isn't just some invisible thing ticking away in the background. It's a dimension, just like the three dimensions of space—length, width, and height. This fourth dimension, time, is woven together with space into a giant cosmic quilt called spacetime. And we're all drifting through this quilt, moving forward in time at one second per second (yes, that's an actual rate of time).

You can move left, right, up, or down in space, but time is a one-way street. You can't just reverse and head back to Tuesday because you forgot it was your grandma's birthday. (Unless you're a time-traveling banana with a PhD in quantum mechanics, which you're probably not.)

So, what does it really mean to "pause time"?

When you say you want to pause time "for yourself," what you're really saying is:

"I want to hit the universal pause button—freeze every atom, every photon, every tick of every clock in existence—and somehow keep my body and brain running like it's just another Tuesday."

That's... a gigantic ask.

Think about it: You're not just freezing your surroundings. You're halting the motion of the entire universe. That includes the molecules in the air, the chemical reactions in plants, the expansion of galaxies, and the flow of energy across all space and time. You're essentially saying, "I want to break the fundamental laws of physics, but just a little bit—and only for me." It's like freezing an entire ocean and expecting one fish (that's you) to keep swimming. A bit unfair to the ocean, don't you think?

And if everything stops—light, air, gravity, sound—what would that mean for you, the lone swimmer? Would you be floating in darkness? Would sound even work without vibrating air molecules? Would your thoughts even happen if the electrical signals in your brain are part of the frozen universe?

Let's go even deeper into this hypothetical mess...

The Science Gets Spicy

Okay, so let's say, hypothetically, you've paused time for everyone and everything except yourself. You can walk, breathe, think, and function normally. Now, here's where science starts asking annoying but important questions.

Breathing Becomes a Problem

If time has stopped, then air molecules are frozen too. That means... no air movement. No oxygen entering your lungs. That's right. Unless you want your magical time-pausing adventure to turn into a very short choking session, you'll need to find a way to generate your own oxygen.

"But wait!" you say. "I'll carry a tank of oxygen!"

Okay, sure. But what about exhaling? That CO_2 has nowhere to go. So congratulations! You've just created your own suffocating gas bubble.

Let's tweak the fantasy a little: Time is paused for everything except you and anything you're touching. That way, your air tank works. But then you'll need to carry a LOT of stuff just to survive. Food, water, clothes, your Wi-Fi router...

No Heat for You

Here's another thing: Heat is molecular movement. If time is frozen, molecules can't move. So... everything becomes absolutely cold. As in near absolute zero — that's -273.15°C, where atoms stop moving.

You're basically strolling through a cosmic freezer, with icicles forming on your eyelashes. You'll need an insanely advanced suit — the kind not even NASA has — just to survive.

So let's revise again: Time is paused for the world, but molecules in your suit and your supplies can move. That way, you don't become a human popsicle.

Light? Nope.

Here's where things get wild.

Light is a wave that travels through space at around 300,000 km/s. If time is paused, light stops too. That means — NO LIGHT. You're now stuck in pitch-blackness. Your eyes can't see anything because light isn't bouncing off objects anymore.

A flashlight? Doesn't work either — light can't "travel" without time.

So, unless you're part bat or have sonar vision, good luck navigating the frozen world without stubbing your toe every two steps.

Let's Take a Break (from Reality)

So, we've already hit the pause button on science and logic. We've activated "Time-Bypass Mode," which basically turns you into the only person on Earth who can live, breathe, blink, and binge-eat nachos while the rest of the universe takes an eternal nap.

At first, it's thrilling. You're the main character in the ultimate solo adventure. No deadlines. No drama. No noise. Just... you.

Sounds perfect? Let's dig deeper.

The Loneliness Level: Expert Mode

Let's face it — most of us dream of alone time. A break from people, pressure, and school bells. But total aloneness? That's a different beast. At first, it feels like a superpower. You run through empty malls, wear whatever you want from fancy stores, high-five frozen pigeons, and ride a rollercoaster without waiting in line (okay, you still have to power it manually, but let's not get technical).

But then the silence sets in.

The kind that makes your ears ring. The kind where you start missing things you didn't think you liked — your friend's bad jokes, the chaos of the school corridor, even your math teacher's complicated chalkboard equations. (Okay, maybe not that much.)

You start talking to statues. You name trees. You debate politics with your reflection. One day you catch yourself throwing a surprise birthday party... for a frozen squirrel.

Learning Alone, Forever

Here's a weird twist: with all that time on your hands, you could become the smartest person alive. Literally.

Read every book? Check. Learn to code? Easy. Build a spaceship? Why not?

But without anyone to share your discoveries with, what's the point? You could write the solution to world hunger on a napkin and leave it in someone's frozen hand... but until time unfreezes, it's just a really smart napkin.

And let's not forget: no internet. Servers are frozen. Wi-Fi is down. You're basically living in the world's largest offline mode.

You can't even Google how to restart time. Now that's tragic.

Ultimate Creativity... with Zero Feedback

You'd have endless time to explore creativity: write a novel, compose music, build a life-size dragon out of soda cans. You can finally finish that dream project. But the applause? The feedback? The high-fives? Nonexistent. Even if you make the greatest work of art in human history, no one else will see it — not until/unless you unpause the world.

So, the question becomes: Would you still do great things if no one ever saw them?

That's a deep one. Take your time. (You've got plenty.)

Welcome to Existential Crisis Café

Let's really think about it: If time moves only for you, are you even part of the same reality anymore?

It's like being a ghost among the living. You exist, you move, you grow... but the world is stuck in a loop, like a paused movie you can't rewind or fast-forward.

Everyone else is frozen in a moment. You're drifting endlessly, like a leaf in a still lake. One day you look in the mirror and realize you've aged. Your face has changed. Your mind has matured. But your friends? Your family? They're exactly as they were the day you hit "pause."

Would you still feel connected to them? Would you still feel... you?

So... Could We Ever Pause Time?

Let's snap back to reality.

Here's the science-y truth:

Stopping time completely breaks the known laws of the universe. Like, crash-the-system level breaks. The laws of motion, entropy, light, energy — all go out the window.

Even if we could pause time, we'd need some way to step outside of spacetime itself. That's like trying to lift yourself off the ground by pulling your shoelaces. Not happening.

Relativity gives us cool tricks like slowing down time (think: black holes, light-speed travel), but pausing it? Sorry. We're not there. And we might never be.

But hey — that's not necessarily a bad thing.

Final Thoughts: Time Is the Ultimate Multiplayer Game

As a student, my days are packed — school, homework, guitar practice, exams, maybe a little existential pondering before bed. Sometimes, I wish I could freeze time just to catch my breath.

But then I think: maybe what makes time special is that it keeps going. It's the great equalizer. We all get the same 24 hours — no pause buttons, no rewinds. What matters is how we use those hours.

We can waste them, race through them, or really live them.

Pausing time might give us freedom — but it takes away connection. It gives us silence — but steals all the music. It hands us endless moments — but no shared memories.

And honestly? I'd rather laugh with my friends, mess up a test, sing off-key, and keep moving forward — with everyone else.

Because living in real time is scary, unpredictable, chaotic...

...and absolutely amazing.

So next time you wish to pause time, maybe just pause your phone, take a breath, and be present.

That's not science fiction. That's just good advice.

And who knows? Maybe learning to live in the moment is the real superpower.

VI

What If The Internet Vanished Overnight?

Unimaginable, right? What's this world today without the internet? Are YOU without internet? Hasn't the internet woven itself too complicatedly in our lives? What if the internet actually vanished? Completely disappeared from our lives?

Let's find out.

Let's say you go to bed after binge-watching videos of cats jumping off kitchen counters. You drift off to sleep, phone on your chest, Wi-Fi signal glowing strong. And then... poof! Gone. Not your cat. Not your phone. But the INTERNET. The mighty web. The lifeline of modern civilization. Gone overnight. As in: 404 Not Found—for real.

You wake up the next morning. Your alarm didn't ring because it was set on a cloud-based app. Strange. Your smart speaker isn't responding. No morning playlist. No

"Today's weather is partly sunny with a 20% chance of forgetting your umbrella." Nothing. You check your phone. No WhatsApp messages. Instagram says, "Couldn't refresh feed." You restart the Wi-Fi router—three times—like a true digital warrior. Still nothing.

Then it hits you.

The internet has vanished.

1. *The World Freezes (Literally and Figuratively)*

Without the internet, communication halts. No emails. No Zoom calls. No Google Meet classes (okay, that part may sound like a dream). But more seriously, most financial systems stop working. ATMs can't connect to banks. UPI, GPay, and PayTM show you spinning wheels of doom. Even swiping your card at the grocery store? Nope. Denied.

Social media? Dead. Online gaming? Gone. Streaming? Forget Netflix and chill. Just... chill. Alone. With your own thoughts. Terrifying, I know.

Meanwhile, back at the local power station, technicians realize they can't remotely monitor the electric grid. Many systems today are internet-reliant, including how we distribute electricity. Not instantly, but gradually, this can lead to overloads, blackouts, and chaos. Hospitals lose access to cloud-based patient records. GPS? Say goodbye to Google Maps—you'll need an actual paper map, which is basically ancient wizardry at this point. (Sounds like some part of a fictional movie, right?)

Even meteorologists can't download the latest satellite data. So, if a thunderstorm is coming your way... surprise!

2. *The Digital Panic Begins (Extended)*

By now, the world's population is split into two groups:

Group A: People panicking because their influencer post didn't get uploaded at 9:00 AM sharp. "My aesthetic feed is RUINED," screams a girl with glitter eyeliner. "This was my viral moment!" cries a boy mid-dance move. Ring lights are switched off in defeat.

Group B: Governments and corporations in emergency meetings yelling, "WHAT. JUST. HAPPENED?"

Stock markets can't function. Trading floors look like chaotic birthday parties—lots of shouting, no music, and zero coordination. Servers across the globe are silent, blinking sadly like forgotten toasters. Cryptocurrency? Gone. Poof. (Bitcoin bros crying in blockchain.)

Tech giants are losing money by the second. CEOs who once wore sneakers and gave TED Talks now look like they've aged a decade in an hour.

News broadcasters, unable to stream feeds or check online scripts, turn back to... faxes. Yes, those ancient whirring machines from the land before time. One anchor holds up a blurry faxed image of a cat meme, trying to make sense of it. "Is this... breaking news?"

Meanwhile, schools around the world have accidentally discovered the most powerful force of nature: Bored Teenagers Without Wi-Fi.

Some try to send messages through Bluetooth, only to find its range is the size of their living room. Group chats fall apart. Emojis become extinct. The real horror begins when someone says: "Let's go outside and talk... you know... in person."

There's an eerie silence on streets once filled with notification pings and Spotify playlists. Now, people walk around dazed, holding their dead phones like they're Tamagotchis that forgot to eat.

Teachers frantically dig up old chalkboards. Parents raid attics looking for board games. Kids attempt to "Google something" and end up staring at their screens with the cute dino-game everyone loves.

3. The First 24 Hours: Chaos and Denial

Phones still work—kind of. Basic SMS and calling are still up, because thankfully, cellular towers don't care about the internet. But the moment someone tries to open WhatsApp, Telegram, or Discord, they're met with the horrifying spinning wheel of doom.

People go to offices out of sheer habit, clutching their coffee like battle armor—only to realize they can't log in to anything. Google Workspace? Blank. Microsoft Azure? Gone. Slack? Silenced. "Remote work" becomes "no work." Zoom calls? Zoom who?

In the brief pause before total panic, students celebrate—no online classes, no assignments, no Google Classroom. They do a little happy dance in their pajamas. Until teachers show up wielding the most ancient and terrifying weapon of all time: printed homework. Handwritten. On paper. With staples. Some kids faint. Others scream. The trees begin weeping silently in the distance.

Meanwhile, the world's digital heartbeat—e-commerce—flatlines. No Amazon. No Flipkart. No Myntra, Nykaa, BigBasket. Your emergency midnight order of pineapple pizza and garlic bread? Cancelled. (Also: why were you ordering that in the first place?)

And the real tragedy? The fall of the mighty 10-minute delivery apps.

Blinkit, Zepto, and Instamart—once the superheroes of modern hunger—are now helpless icons on a frozen home screen. Somewhere in a neighborhood, a teenager is dramatically whispering: "I clicked... and it didn't blink."

Hungry people stare out their balconies, hoping to spot a Zepto rider. But the streets are empty. No buzzing scooters. No paper bags filled with iced tea and overpriced bananas.

Panic sets in.

Parents are forced to—brace yourself—cook. Children stand in shock as kitchens come alive again. Gas stoves roar. Pressure cookers whistle. Dads ask where the salt is.

And those who can't cook? They descend into chaos. Cereal and ketchup become dinner. Someone starts eating raw Maggi straight out of the pack (Believe me, I've done that).

No internet. No instant delivery. Just hunger, printer paper, and the creeping feeling that this "little outage" might not be so little after all.

And me? I'm journaling all of it—because if the world ends, someone's gotta write the documentary.

4. What About Science, Tech, and Space?

Here's the scarier part: the internet isn't just about memes and online shopping. It's also how scientists communicate data, how researchers collaborate, and how satellites relay critical climate information.

Astronomers can't download data from space telescopes.

Engineers can't update software on interplanetary missions.

Rocket launches? Suspended, unless controlled entirely offline.

Even scientific journals are published online. Imagine a PhD student screaming into the void because they can't access "Nature.com." Tragic.

But not everything is doomed—some high-security systems still use local networks or independent intranets (tiny internal networks not connected to the public internet). So a few smart labs can still function, but collaboration becomes letters and landlines.

5. Could This Actually Happen?

Okay, let's switch gears. Is this even possible?

Technically... yes, but not easily.

The internet is decentralized. There's no single off-switch, like a giant red button labeled "INTERNET: ON/OFF." (Although that would be cool—and terrifying.) But it can be disrupted on large scales.

Examples:

In 2008, a ship's anchor accidentally cut an underwater internet cable near Egypt, causing widespread outages in the Middle East and India.

Countries like North Korea and Iran have restricted or even shut down internet access during crises.

Solar storms—bursts of electromagnetic energy from the Sun—can damage satellites and power grids, which may disrupt the internet globally.

And then there's cyberwarfare. A well-coordinated attack could take down critical DNS (Domain Name System) servers, hijack routers, or overload cloud providers. It's difficult, but not impossible. The biggest risk? Human error. A bad software update could mess up vast portions of the net.

6. Life Without Internet: Rewind Time

Let's imagine this isn't just a one-day glitch but a permanent situation. What happens?

a. Communication

Welcome back to the golden age of SMS, radio, and (brace yourself) landline phones. Fax machines may rise from the grave like zombies.

b. Education

No YouTube tutorials. No Khan Academy. No Google. Students will have to use... books. Libraries will finally get the attention they deserve. (Dusts off Britannica Encyclopedia Volume L). People will start using dictionaries (Imagine sitting 2 hours to search for the meaning of a word, which you could do in 2 second on google).

Teachers start assigning handwritten projects. Students start sobbing in cursive.

c. Entertainment

People rediscover board games. Grandparents tell dad jokes in person. Families actually talk at dinner. Wild.

Teenagers start recording videos on their phones for no one but themselves, like some kind of digital journaling. "Hey guys, day 42 without internet. I've befriended a pigeon. He's my only subscriber now."

d. Business and Economy

The global economy takes a historic hit. E-commerce dies. Digital banking collapses. Small offline businesses rise again—those old mom-and-pop stores become lifelines. People trade cash. Bartering makes a comeback. "I'll give you three eggs for that phone charger."

Companies scramble to build local intranets. Paper resumes return. So do face-to-face interviews. (Introverts collectively faint.)

e. Innovation

Surprisingly, innovation doesn't die. It just slows down. Scientists start meeting in person more often. Research labs use offline systems. People begin inventing new, offline ways of doing things—like mesh networks or local servers. As they say – Necessity is the mother of invention.

Tech companies rush to develop a new version of the internet. Let's call it InterNot 2.0—a slower, locally hosted, community-based network. Kind of like internet villages.

7. Unexpected Benefits

Believe it or not, there are some upsides.

No more scrolling at 2 a.m.

No cyberbullying.

No spam emails, pop-up ads, or online scams.

People might sleep better.

We stop comparing our lives to filtered Instagram posts.

And maybe—just maybe—we reconnect with the real world.

Parks are full. People actually look up. Artists, writers, and musicians find peace without algorithms chasing them.

Also, pigeons become popular again for sending messages. "Hey bro, text me your pigeon's name."

8. Could We Build It Back?

Absolutely. But it would take years.

First, rebuild physical infrastructure—fiber-optic cables, satellites, data centers.

Second, write the software again. Reinstall systems, reboot servers, reprogram routers.

And most importantly: secure it. Make sure the new internet is stronger, safer, and maybe... less addictive?

Some propose local networks instead of one giant global one. Others want digital balance—part offline, part online. A new internet, but with brakes.

Final Thoughts

The internet disappearing overnight would be one of the greatest shocks to modern civilization. It would collapse economies, freeze communication, and disrupt nearly every aspect of our lives—from science to schooling to the humble act of ordering pizza at midnight.

But maybe—just maybe—it would remind us of what really matters: people, connection, creativity, and pigeons with cute messenger bags.

In a world where we measure time in Wi-Fi bars and productivity in email replies, maybe losing the internet—even temporarily—could act like a giant reboot button for humanity. A forced log-out from the cloud to reconnect us with the ground. We'd be nudged—okay, shoved—into re-learning how to be human without the screen acting as a medium.

We'd read more, talk more, maybe even walk more—mainly because Google Maps isn't saving us from our horrendous sense of direction. We'd write letters, keep diaries, and find joy in slowness. That buzzing tension in your brain, the one that twitches every time a notification pings? It would start to fade. You'd begin to feel what silence actually sounds like.

Our generation, the so-called "digital natives," would go through the toughest withdrawal. No memes, no reels, no "guess who viewed your story?" suspense. But we might also become the most innovative—forced to reimagine how to connect, learn, and share without Wi-Fi. New offline inventions would rise. Maybe we'd finally figure out how to build a digital app that doesn't need the internet to work.

And hey, schools would start teaching practical things again—like using a compass that doesn't require GPS or writing without autocorrect.

Yes, we'd lose a lot. But we'd also gain something rare in today's world: presence. Awareness. Eye contact without emojis. Conversations without buffering. Friendships not measured in followers, but in footsteps taken together.

In the end, the internet is a tool. A powerful one. But tools are meant to help us build a better life, not become the life itself.

So maybe, if it ever vanishes—just for a day or forever—we'll learn to look up more often. To listen more. To laugh without filters. To rediscover the magic of a lazy afternoon with nothing but a book, a breeze, and maybe... a pigeon with a message.

And who knows? If the internet ever does come back, maybe we won't use it just to scroll.

Maybe we'll use it to truly connect.

VII

What If We Lived Underwater Instead Of On Land?

Imagine waking up one day and realizing you don't live on land anymore. No more streets, no more parks, no more sky. Instead, your entire world is underwater. You brush your teeth surrounded by fish, your school is a giant coral reef, and your morning commute involves swimming past a school of dolphins. Sounds like a sci-fi movie, right? But what if humans actually lived underwater instead of on land? What would life be like? Would we still have smartphones, or would we have to invent underwater versions? Could we breathe? And how would science explain all this?

Let's dive deep into this fascinating question and explore the science behind living underwater, the challenges we'd face, and maybe even some cool perks.

The Basic Problem: Humans Can't Breath Underwater

First thing's first: humans can't breathe underwater. Our lungs are designed to extract oxygen from air, not water. Fish and other sea creatures have gills—special organs that pull oxygen dissolved in water—while we rely on air with roughly 21% oxygen. Our respiratory system simply isn't built for the dense, oxygen-poor environment underwater.

If we lived underwater, breathing would be our biggest problem. Unless you're a scuba diver with a tank (which only lasts a few hours and is super bulky), you can't just hold your breath forever. The average human can hold their breath for about 30 seconds to 2 minutes—far too short to survive beneath the waves. Even the most skilled free divers train for years to push this limit to around 10 minutes or so, but that's still just a fraction of the time you'd need to live underwater regularly.

So, how could we solve this? Here are some possibilities:

Gills? If humans had evolved gills, we could breathe underwater like fish. But that would require huge evolutionary changes in our bodies. Our noses and mouths would have to change to accommodate water flow, and our entire respiratory system would be different. Fish gills work by extracting tiny amounts of dissolved oxygen from water as it flows past them, but they require a very different anatomy. Imagine if instead of our current lungs, we had feathery gills extending from our necks, filtering oxygen directly from water. However, this raises questions about how we would breathe air on land or how our brains and blood systems would adapt to such a major change. Evolution takes millions of years, and such adaptations would likely come only if humans lived underwater for many generations.

Oxygen tanks and equipment: Maybe we'd invent lightweight, built-in breathing devices like sci-fi superheroes. Imagine a tiny gadget embedded in your neck or chest, constantly supplying oxygen, much like an invisible scuba tank. Instead of lugging bulky gear, it would allow you to swim freely, talk, and interact underwater without restrictions. Scientists and engineers are already working on compact rebreather systems that recycle exhaled air, making breathing equipment smaller and more efficient. Perhaps in the future, wearable tech could even extract oxygen from the water itself, eliminating the need for bulky tanks.

Water-breathing technology: Researchers are exploring artificial gills—devices that mimic fish gills by extracting oxygen directly from water. These gadgets would let divers stay underwater for hours or even days without surfacing. Although current prototypes are bulky and not yet practical, the potential is huge. If perfected, artificial gills could revolutionize underwater exploration, allowing humans to live, work, or even build cities beneath the ocean. Picture underwater habitats where people swim freely, breathing through tiny devices hidden under their skin or clothing.

Other creative solutions: What if humans could hold their breath for hours? Or develop a symbiotic relationship with aquatic creatures that provide oxygen? Maybe underwater cities will have air pockets and tunnels filled with breathable air, connected by transparent domes, allowing humans to live underwater without needing to breathe water at all.

In short, while humans can't naturally breathe underwater, science and technology might one day bridge the gap. Whether through artificial gills, advanced breathing gear, genetic tweaks, or something we haven't even imagined yet, the dream of living beneath the waves could become reality. Until then, we'll have to stick to surface air and our trusty scuba tanks.

Our Bodies Underwater: What Would Change?

Living underwater isn't just about breathing. Our bodies would face other big challenges too.

Pressure, Pressure, Pressure!

Water is heavy. The deeper you go underwater, the more pressure there is. For every 10 meters you dive, the pressure increases by about 1 atmosphere (the pressure we feel at sea level). If we lived deep underwater, our bodies would have to deal with crushing pressures that could squash us like a pancake.

Deep-sea creatures have adapted to this by having flexible bones or no bones at all, and special proteins that prevent damage. Humans, however, have rigid bones and air-filled cavities (lungs, sinuses) that would collapse under high pressure.

If we lived underwater, we'd probably have to live close to the surface—like in shallow seas or specially designed habitats—to avoid these dangers.

Temperature and Warmth

Water conducts heat away from our bodies about 25 times faster than air. That means underwater, we'd get cold really fast. Most fish and sea animals are cold-blooded, meaning their body temperature matches the water. Humans are warm-blooded, so we'd need to find ways to keep warm.

That could mean wearing high-tech insulating suits or evolving thicker skin or blubber like whales and seals. Otherwise, we'd be shivering all day!

Moving Around

Walking on land is easy, but swimming is a whole different story. Our limbs aren't designed for underwater movement like fins or flippers. We'd have to get good at swimming to get anywhere.

Maybe we'd evolve webbed fingers and toes, stronger muscles, or even a tail for propulsion. Or perhaps underwater vehicles would be our "cars," zooming us through the ocean. Who knows?

How Would Our Homes Look?

Imagine living underwater—what kind of houses would we have?

Underwater Cities

We couldn't just build normal houses; the pressure and water would crush them. Instead, we'd need waterproof, pressure-resistant habitats. Think of giant domes made of super-strong glass or special metals, keeping water out and air in.

Scientists today are already exploring underwater habitats for research. For example, the Aquarius Reef Base is a real underwater lab off the coast of Florida, where scientists live and work for weeks at a time.

In the future, we might build underwater cities like those in movies such as Aquaman. These cities would have:

Air-filled zones with comfortable temperatures

Airlocks to enter and exit water safely

Special windows for viewing sea life

Underwater farms growing algae or seaweed for food

Food Underwater

How would we eat? Farming underwater is tricky but possible. Seaweed, algae, and certain fish can be farmed underwater. Shellfish like oysters and mussels are already farmed on the ocean floor. (Tiny problem for the vegetarians, isn't it?)

We might develop underwater hydroponic gardens to grow fruits and vegetables in special pods or tanks. Protein sources would mostly be fish or other seafood.

What About Light and Sound?

Seeing Underwater

Light underwater is like that one friend who always leaves the party early — the reds and yellows vanish quickly as you dive deeper. Water loves to gobble up warm colors first, leaving everything with a bluish or greenish tint.

If humans lived underwater, our eyes would have to get a serious upgrade. Maybe we'd develop night-vision goggles built right into our eyeballs, like those nocturnal sea creatures who don't blink twice at pitch-black depths. Or better yet, imagine if we evolved bioluminescence — basically glowing like underwater disco balls — to help us see and say, "Hey, over here!" in style. Just picture underwater dance parties lit by human glowsticks.

Sound Travels Faster

Sound is a speed demon underwater — it travels about 4.5 times faster than in air. That means voices would sound like they're running a marathon, and your underwater gossip might turn into a confusing blur of echoes. So, your underwater "hello" might come across as a mysterious dolphin whistle or a submarine sonar ping. Forget about shouting; you'd probably have to master clicking noises or vibrations just to say, "Pass the seaweed salad."

Communication might get pretty creative. Instead of awkward conversations, you could have flashing light signals like Morse code or maybe a full-on underwater light show every time you want to share a secret.

What About Our Culture and Daily Life?

Sports and Fun

No more football fields or basketball courts underwater! Sports would change completely. Imagine underwater swimming races, dolphin rides, or bubble volleyball.

Music might sound different, and instruments would have to be waterproof or use water vibrations.

Clothes and Fashion

Regular clothes wouldn't work underwater. We'd wear special suits that keep us warm and allow us to move freely. Maybe future fashion designers would create sleek, shiny wetsuits or glowing accessories.

Transportation

Walking? Forget it. We'd swim or use submarines and underwater scooters. Highways might be lanes marked with light signals, guiding underwater vehicles.

What Does Science Say?

Humans Are Not Built for Underwater Living

From an evolutionary standpoint, humans evolved on land for millions of years. Our lungs, skin, bones, and metabolism are adapted to air breathing, walking upright, and temperature regulation on land. Humans have survived short periods underwater using scuba gear, free diving, and submarine technology—but full-time underwater living isn't currently feasible.

Marine Mammals Show It's Possible

Whales, dolphins, seals, and otters live in water but are still mammals—they breathe air. They've evolved amazing adaptations like:

Holding breath for long periods (dolphins up to 15 minutes)

Streamlined bodies for swimming

Thick blubber for insulation

If humans lived underwater, maybe we'd develop some similar traits over thousands of years.

What About Future Tech?

Scientists and engineers are developing underwater habitats for research and maybe even tourism or colonization. These habitats could be the first step toward living underwater. Artificial gills, exosuits, and underwater vehicles could make it easier for humans to explore and maybe live in underwater environments someday.

Fun Facts and Figures

- The ocean covers about 71% of Earth's surface but humans live mostly on land.
- The deepest part of the ocean, the Mariana Trench, is about 11 kilometers deep—pressure there is over 1,000 times what we experience on the surface!
- Some fish can breathe air, like the lungfish, which can survive months out of water.
- Free divers can hold their breath for over 10 minutes underwater!
- The largest underwater habitat ever built for humans is the Aquarius Reef Base, 19 meters below the surface, with a capacity for 6 people.
- Humans have walked on land for over 6 million years but have only explored about 5% of the ocean.

Wrapping Up: Would You Want to Live Underwater?

Living underwater sounds exciting—swimming with fish, exploring coral reefs, and discovering new underwater worlds. But it also comes with big challenges: breathing, pressure, cold, and darkness.

Maybe in the future, with advances in technology and biology, humans might live underwater for short periods or in special habitats. But for now, the ocean remains a mysterious and beautiful place where only specially adapted creatures can truly call home.

So, if you ever feel like you're drowning in homework, just imagine living underwater—where even breathing could be a struggle! Probably better to stick to land for now.

What do you think? Would you want to swap your house for a coral reef? Or are you happy with dry land and fresh air?

VIII

What If All Insects Vanished Tomorrow?

That would be such a relief, wouldn't it? No more troublesome mosquitoes biting off our skin here and there. But it isn't as happy and joyful you think it might be. Why? Aren't insects just a side character in the story of our lives? Aren't they the tiny troublemakers that suck our blood up?

No. It' not just that.

Why?

Let's find out.

First Things First: How Many Insects Are There?

Short answer: Way more than you think.

Long answer: Hold on to your bug spray.

Scientists estimate there are around 10 quintillion insects on Earth at any given time. That's a 1 followed by 19 zeros. Written out, it looks like this:

    10,000,000,000,000,000,000.

(Go ahead, count the zeros. I'll wait.)

To give you an idea of how mind-blowing that number is, there are only about 8 billion humans on the planet. So for every one of us, there are 1.25 billion insects. That means if insects ever got organized and held a protest march, you wouldn't just be outnumbered—you'd be swarmed.

And insects aren't just extra players in the cast of life on Earth—they're basically running the show behind the scenes. Think of them as the ultimate backstage crew for Planet Earth. They pollinate flowers, recycle nutrients, clean up dead things (gross, but helpful), and are a major food source for countless other animals. Some even farm (like leafcutter ants), build architecture (hello, termite mounds), or perform aerial acrobatics that would make fighter pilots jealous.

Insects come in an almost absurd variety of shapes and sizes. There are beetles so shiny they look chrome-plated, butterflies that migrate thousands of kilometers with no GPS, and wasps that lay eggs inside other insects like something straight out of a sci-fi horror movie. Some glow in the dark, some can walk on water, and some even explode (seriously—look up bombardier beetles).

In fact, about 80% of all animal species on Earth are insects. That means if you picked a random animal from the planet's biosphere, chances are very high it would have six legs, an exoskeleton, and possibly a strange fondness for your picnic lunch.

So, if they all vanished overnight, we're not just losing a few buzzing annoyances or the reason we sometimes wave our hands wildly in summer. We're erasing most of the life forms on Earth in one swift snap. No more bees to pollinate crops. No more dung beetles to clean up messes. No more silk from silkworms, no more honey from bees, and no more butterflies to remind us that nature still exists.

It wouldn't just be a bugpocalypse (bug + apocalypse, just in case you're wondering)—it'd be an ecological disaster. Forests would suffer. Food chains would collapse. Crops would fail. Many birds, reptiles, amphibians, and mammals would struggle to survive. And eventually? So would we.

Insects may be tiny, but when it comes to keeping the planet running smoothly, they're giants.

Problem #1: Who's Going to Pollinate Our Food?

Let's start with your breakfast.

That juicy apple? Thank the bees.

The almonds in your granola? Bee job.

The chocolate in your muffin? Midges (tiny, midge-sized pollinators).

Your cup of coffee? You guessed it—bees again.

Over 75% of flowering plants and about one-third of the food we eat depend on insects for pollination. That includes fruits, veggies, nuts, spices, and even chocolate. Without these pollinators, your plate would look... very brown and very boring.

Could humans take over the job? Technically, yes. People have tried hand-pollinating flowers using tiny brushes and cotton swabs. But it takes thousands of people to do what a small swarm of bees can accomplish in one afternoon. And it costs a lot. You want a ₹1000 an apple? Neither do we.

And bees aren't just helpful—they're valuable. No bees = no pollination = no apples, no almonds, no avocados, and definitely no chocolate.

What's left? Mostly wind-pollinated crops like wheat, corn, and rice.

Yum... plain rice every day for life.

Problem #2: Insects Are the Planet's Janitors

Okay, real talk—bugs deal with the gross stuff, so we don't have to.

Think of the forest. What happens when a squirrel dies? Or a pile of poop is left behind? Or a tree drops its leaves?

Insects jump in to clean it up.

Dung beetles roll poop into balls and bury it. (Some can roll up to 50 times their own weight!)

Carrion beetles and fly larvae eat dead animals.

Ants and termites break down fallen leaves and dead wood.

Without these cleanup crews, all that waste would just sit there. Forever. It would pile up, rot, and stink. And rotting stuff attracts bacteria and disease. Basically, Earth would start to smell like the world's worst garbage dump. Yuck.

Problem #3: Animals Would Starve

Let's say you're a bird. You wake up, hungry for some crunchy caterpillars. You look around... but nothing's moving. No bugs at all.

Bad news.

Insects are a major food source for birds, frogs, lizards, fish, bats—even mammals like anteaters, armadillos, and bears (yes, bears eat bugs too). If insects disappeared, many of these animals would lose their food source and starve.

Then the animals that eat those animals would go hungry. And so on. It's like removing the first domino in a long line. Everything falls.

Within weeks, entire ecosystems could start to collapse. Forests would go quiet. Rivers would lose their fish. The skies would be empty of birds. Life would unravel.

Problem #4: Soil Would Stop Being Awesome

We walk on it every day, but soil is actually alive. It's full of bacteria, fungi, worms—and insects.

Insects like ants, beetles, and springtails (tiny, jumpy soil bugs) help by:

Digging tunnels that let air and water flow underground

Breaking down dead plants and animals into nutrients

Moving those nutrients through the soil

Without them, the soil becomes hard and dry. Plants can't grow as well. Crops suffer. Trees weaken. Even oxygen levels might drop because fewer plants would be photosynthesizing.

So yes—bugs help you breathe.

Problem #5: No More Butterflies, Fireflies, or Buzzing Nights

Now let's talk about the pretty side of bugs.

If insects vanished, we'd lose:

Butterflies dancing in gardens

Fireflies glowing in the summer night

Beetles with shiny, rainbow shells

Moths with wings like velvet paintings

Dragonflies doing loop-the-loops around ponds

These insects aren't just for decoration. They're signs that an ecosystem is healthy and alive. Without them, Earth would be a quieter, duller, lonelier place. No buzzing. No chirping. Just silence.

You might think that sounds peaceful. Until you realize it means everything else—plants, animals, forests—is gone too.

But Wait—Wouldn't There Be Some Upsides?

Alright, let's be fair. If insects disappeared, some annoying things would stop:

No more mosquito bites

No more cockroaches in the kitchen

No more flies landing on your food

But these "wins" are like getting rid of school but also losing books, friends, snacks, and sports.

Even the annoying insects play a part:

Mosquitoes feed fish, birds, and bats. (Also, only females bite. Males just sip flower nectar.)

Cockroaches help break down waste in tropical forests.

Flies pollinate, decompose, and feed other animals.

So yeah, they might bug you—but they also help you.

Could Humans Survive?

If insects disappeared completely and suddenly?

Probably not. Pollination would stop. Crops would fail. Waste would pile up. Animals would starve. Ecosystems would collapse. Disease might spread faster. Air and food would be in short supply.

The United Nations already warns that insect declines are a serious threat to global food security. And that's just from a gradual drop—not an instant vanishing.

We rely on insects more than we realize. Without them, the whole system breaks.

Are Insects Really in Danger?

Sadly, yes.

Studies show that insect numbers are falling fast. In some places, 75% of insects have disappeared in just a few decades. That's terrifying.

Why?

Pesticides kill both pests and helpful bugs

Deforestation and farming destroy habitats

Climate change messes with insect life cycles

Pollution harms bugs directly

Invasive species outcompete local insects

So no, they haven't all vanished. But they're disappearing. Quietly. Quickly. And we need to act now.

What Can We Do?

The good news? We can make a difference.

Plant Native Flowers

Even a few pots on a balcony can help pollinators.

Avoid Harmful Pesticides

Use natural methods when possible. Let bugs do their job.

Support Organic Farms

They use insect-friendly techniques and avoid chemicals.

Build Bug Hotels

These mini-shelters give insects a place to rest and lay eggs.

Respect the Little Guys

Even if they crawl. Even if they buzz. Even if they're weird-looking.

Final Thoughts: The Bug Truth

So... what if all insects vanished tomorrow?

At first, you'd cheer. No bites. No buzz. No bugs.

Then you'd notice the apples are gone.

Then the waste piles up.

Then the birds vanish.

Then the plants start dying.

And finally—so might we.

Insects may be tiny, but they're mighty. They pollinate, decompose, feed, build, breathe, and balance life on Earth. Without them, the whole web of life starts to fall apart.

So next time you see a bee in your garden, a moth at your window, or a beetle on your shoe, don't squash it.

Salute it (Okay, that might be a bit too much but at least don't kill it).

Because hey! It's holding up the world.

IX

What If You Could Upload Your Brain To A Computer?

Imagine this: You're sitting on your bed, textbook open, eyes heavy from reading about amoebas for the third time. You sigh, look up at the ceiling, and whisper:

"What if I could just upload all this into my brain... or better, upload my brain into a computer?"

Well, first of all—congrats. You're now officially a participant in one of the coolest and creepiest thought experiments of the 21st century. It's called mind uploading or whole brain emulation, and it's the idea that we could, theoretically, transfer the contents of your brain—your thoughts, memories, personality, weird obsessions, math trauma, and all—into a computer.

Let's dive in (no helmet required) and figure out if this sci-fi fantasy is even remotely possible, and what would happen if it were.

So... What Exactly Is a Brain Upload?

A brain upload would mean making a digital copy of your brain so detailed and accurate that it behaves exactly like you. Not just your memories or thoughts, but your entire consciousness. In simple terms, it's like making a super-detailed PDF of you, but instead of paper, it's stored in code. Like, next-level Google Drive storage for humans.

But here's the catch: your brain isn't just a big sponge that holds facts about periodic tables and random YouTube sounds. It's a massively complex biological organ with over 86 billion neurons, each connecting to about 1,000 others. That's roughly 100 trillion connections, or as we scientists like to say—"a metric buttload."

To upload a brain, scientists would need to map every single one of those neurons and their connections (called the connectome) and then replicate how they behave electrically and chemically inside a computer. So far, the only brain we've fully mapped is... drumroll please... the brain of a roundworm.

Yes. A worm. With just 302 neurons.

The Science Bit (a.k.a. "Will This Ever Be Real?")

Alright, it's time to pop the hood on this wild idea of brain uploading and see what's really going on under there. Because while science fiction loves to tell us we're just a few brilliant nerds and a dramatic lightning storm away from uploading ourselves into the cloud, real science has a checklist that's... slightly more intense. Let's break it down:

1. Crazy-Precise Brain Scanning Technology

First things first: before you can upload a brain, you need to understand every single microscopic detail about it. That means creating a map so detailed it tracks every neuron, every synapse, every chemical, and every electrical zap that sparks when you remember where you left your socks.

That sounds cool—until you realize that current brain-mapping technology is a bit like trying to draw a city map using a telescope from the Moon. Sure, we're making progress. Scientists at places like the Allen Institute for Brain Science are literally mapping mouse brains one cell at a time, which is a Herculean task by itself. But a mouse brain is about the size of a peanut. A human brain? That's around 86 billion neurons, each with 10,000 connections. Multiply that out and your head starts to spin—and we haven't even started scanning yet.

Now here's the kicker: even our best high-resolution brain imaging tools today—like electron microscopes—can only scan dead brains. Not just "recently deceased," but actually sliced apart into ultra-thin layers. The process destroys the brain in order to preserve the data. Which means... yeah, your digital self might wake up, but you won't. That isn't funny, is it?

And let's not forget the storage nightmare. Mapping just one cubic millimeter of brain tissue at nanometer resolution would take up petabytes of storage. To map a whole human brain at that resolution? You'd need more digital storage than currently exists on Earth. Better start saving up for a few exabytes of external hard drives.

2. Ridiculous Computer Power (Your Brain > All Supercomputers)

Let's say—miracle of miracles—you managed to scan a whole brain in glorious molecular detail. Now you have to simulate it. In real-time. All of it.

The human brain is freakishly efficient. It runs on about 20 watts of power—less than a dim light bulb—but it can outthink every supercomputer we've ever built. That's because your brain is running 100 trillion synaptic operations per second, and it does it without crashing, overheating, or needing a firmware update.

To digitally model that level of activity, we'd need supercomputers capable of petaflops of processing power (that's a quadrillion calculations per second).

Also, storage. Again. All the info in a human brain adds up to around 2.5 petabytes—that's 2.5 million gigabytes, or roughly 300,000 hours of HD Netflix streaming. And that's just the raw data. If you want backups, simulations, or to run more than one copy of yourself (why not?), you're going to need a cloud plan that makes Google sweat.

3. Software That Understands Consciousness (The Ultimate Coding Challenge)

Here's the most philosophical—and frustrating—part of the whole thing: we don't know what consciousness actually is. We experience it every day. We say, "I think, therefore I am." But what does "I" even mean in the context of code?

Even if we had a perfect scan and the computer power to run it, what would make the upload "you"? Is it just the neural data? The memory banks? The pattern of electrical activity? Or is it something more mysterious—like how all the parts work together in just the right way?

Some scientists believe consciousness arises from emergent complexity—meaning once you simulate the brain closely enough, consciousness might naturally emerge like steam from boiling water. Others think we're missing a key ingredient—something we don't even know we don't know.

And then there's the ultimate stumper: if we did it, would your digital copy feel like you? Or would it be a hollow echo, a brilliant mimic without the inner spark that makes you... you?

Trying to code consciousness right now is like trying to translate Beethoven's Ninth Symphony into spaghetti. It just doesn't compute. We can scan brainwaves, track emotions, even implant false memories in mice—but we can't yet describe what makes someone feel like themselves, much less simulate it.

Okay, But What If We Could Do It?

Let's pretend we cracked it. The year is 2095. You walk into a brain clinic and say, "Upload me, doc." You lie down, the scanner whirrs, and 30 minutes later—bam—you're officially a digital human.

So... what happens next?

You Now Exist in a Computer

Let's call this version Digital You. They look like you (if the simulation has graphics), they talk like you, they remember your dog's name and your childhood traumas with maths.

But here's the twist: You—the biological version—are still lying on the bed. You didn't move. The upload is just a copy. So which one is the real you? This is the classic dilemma. If you make an exact copy of yourself, is that still you, or just a super creepy digital twin?

Want to Live Forever?

Digital You could potentially live forever. No ageing, no diseases, no need for coffee. You could back yourself up on a hard drive, send yourself into space, or live in a Minecraft server for eternity.

But you'd also lose physical experiences—like hugging your best friend, eating pizza, or sneezing seven times in a row and wondering if you're an alien.

What Would Society Look Like?

Uploading brains could totally mess with how we define life and death. Would digital people have rights? Could they vote? Would they get jobs or get taxed? Could your uploaded self go to school for you? (Dream scenario, honestly.)

Also, would only rich people be able to afford it? Because nothing screams dystopia like billionaires living forever as digital clouds while the rest of us are still stuck paying rent.

Fun—and Slightly Terrifying—Possibilities

Digital School

Imagine logging into your virtual classroom—literally as code. No more handwriting assignments. Just merge files with your teacher.

Backup Your Brain

Forgot where you kept your keys? Just load your yesterday save file. Accidentally offended someone? Rewind and pick a different dialogue option. Life becomes an RPG.

Infinite Clones of You

Scary thought: what if someone copied your digital brain a thousand times and made you work in a virtual factory forever? (Hello, Black Mirror.)

Can You Really Be Just Data?

Here's where it gets weird. If your mind is just patterns of information, and we can recreate those perfectly—are you just data?

Some scientists think yes. Your thoughts, memories, and even your sense of self are just neural patterns. If they can be encoded, then you can live in a computer. Others argue that consciousness might require a biological brain—that it emerges from messy, organic chemistry, not clean lines of code.

We don't really know. And that's the wild part.

So… Would You Do It?

Would you upload yourself to a computer if you could?

Would you live forever as a digital being, watching centuries pass? Or would you rather stick to the messy, emotional, inconvenient, wonderful rollercoaster of being a human?

It's a personal choice. And maybe one day, it'll be a real one. But for now, your brain is still snugly inside your skull, doing its 86-billion-neuron thing.

And unless you're a worm, you're safe from uploading—for now.

Final Thought:

If your brain was uploaded… and your digital self is reading this… hello, future you. Hope you're enjoying your 9000th year in the cloud. And if your RAM is starting to feel foggy—maybe you just need a nap. Or a good old system reboot.

Better advice – Stay Human.

X

What If The Earth Was Twice As Big?

Imagine waking up one morning, stretching your arms out, and suddenly noticing—wait a minute! —the horizon looks way farther away, the sky feels a little heavier, and your sneakers seem a bit snugger. Welcome to Earth 2.0—only, it's twice as big! But what does that really mean? Would we still be the same planet we know and love? Or would this super-sized Earth be a totally different ballgame? Let's buckle up and explore this gigantic "what if."

First Things First: What Does "Twice as Big" Even Mean?

When we say "twice as big," what do we really mean? Is it twice the diameter — like measuring straight across the middle from one side to the other? Or is it twice the volume — the amount of space inside the Earth? Because those two are very different things.

Let's break it down.

Earth's diameter is about 12,742 kilometers. So, if Earth's diameter suddenly doubled, it would stretch out to around 25,484 kilometers. Sounds straightforward enough, right? Twice the size across the middle. But here's where it gets wild.

See, volume — the total space inside a sphere like Earth — doesn't just increase in a simple way when you make the diameter bigger. Instead, volume depends on the cube of the radius (which is half the diameter). The formula for the volume of a sphere is:

$$V = \frac{4}{3}\pi r^2$$

If the radius doubles, you cube that factor of 2 — which means the volume becomes 2 *cube*, which is 8 times larger. That's eight times more space inside the planet! So, if Earth's diameter doubles, its volume doesn't just double — it grows eight times bigger.

And what about mass? Well, if we assume the Earth stays just as dense (meaning the amount of stuff packed into each cubic kilometer stays the same), then mass scales with volume. That means the Earth's mass would also increase eightfold.

Gravity: The New Heavyweight Champion

Gravity is the invisible force pulling everything down to Earth's surface. Right now, it's about 9.8 meters per second squared (m/s²). That means if you drop an apple, it accelerates downward at this rate. But what if Earth suddenly had twice the diameter—and eight times the volume and mass?

Here's the science: gravity at the surface depends on Earth's mass and the distance from the center (the radius). The formula is:

$$g = \frac{G \cdot M}{R^2}$$

Where:

G is the gravitational constant

M is the Earth's mass

R is the radius of the earth

If Earth's radius doubles, *r square* becomes 4 times bigger. But Earth's mass becomes 8 times bigger (volume and mass scale together if density stays the same).

So:

$$g_{new} = \frac{G \cdot 8M}{(2R)^2} = \frac{8GM}{4R^2} = 2 \cdot \frac{GM}{R^2} = 2g$$

Boom! Surface gravity doubles. So instead of feeling 9.8 m/s², you'd feel about 19.6 m/s². That's like carrying an extra backpack all the time—except the backpack weighs as much as you do!

What Does This Mean for Us?

Walking would be a workout. Imagine every step requiring twice as much effort. You'd get tired faster, and maybe jogging would turn into a serious sport.

Jumping? Forget about it. Your best jump height would be cut roughly in half.

Buildings, bridges, and everything else would need to be much stronger to hold their own weight.

Atmosphere: Thicker, Denser, and More Breathable?

With more gravity, Earth would hold onto its atmosphere tighter. Right now, some gases like hydrogen and helium escape into space over time because Earth's gravity isn't strong enough to keep the lightest gases.

On a bigger Earth, that escape would be slower. So, the atmosphere might be thicker or denser—meaning air pressure at the surface could be higher. Breathing might feel heavier, almost like climbing a mountain but in reverse.

Weather patterns might change. With a denser atmosphere, wind speeds and storms could get wilder or calmer depending on many factors.

Would humans have trouble breathing? Probably not right away. Our bodies can adjust to different air pressures. But it would definitely feel different—like swimming through air that's a bit thicker.

Plate Tectonics: More Drama Under Your Feet

Earth's surface isn't one solid piece—it's made of huge slabs called tectonic plates that slowly drift around. When these plates bump, slide, or dive under each other, they cause earthquakes, volcanoes, and even build mountain ranges like the Himalayas. It's like the planet's own version of an intense wrestling match.

Now, if Earth suddenly ballooned to twice its diameter—meaning its volume (and likely mass) would jump by a factor of eight—things underground would get way more exciting.

Why?

Because the amount of radioactive elements inside Earth—like uranium, thorium, and potassium—would also increase. These elements decay slowly, releasing heat. This heat warms Earth's mantle, causing the rock there to behave like a super slow-moving lava lamp, driving mantle convection currents that push the tectonic plates.

With eight times the volume, Earth's internal heat generation would be huge. Imagine a planet-sized oven turned way up. This means stronger mantle convection: The "mantle conveyor belt" that moves plates would be more powerful, pushing plates faster and harder. More frequent and intense earthquakes: Plates crashing and sliding would cause more tremors. Forget the occasional shake—this would be earthquake central.

Volcanoes everywhere: With faster mantle convection, molten rock would push up more often, creating volcanoes that might pop up like popcorn kernels in a pot.

Super mountain building: Crashing plates could pile up mountains even faster. Maybe you'd see Himalayan-sized ranges rising in decades instead of millions of years.

But hold on! There's a twist.

As Earth's radius doubles, the pressure and temperature deep inside the core and mantle skyrocket. This extreme pressure changes the way minerals behave—some rocks become denser and less mobile, possibly slowing convection in certain layers. It's a bit like trying to stir a pot of super-thick soup versus regular soup.

So tectonic activity might either speed up or slow down depending on exactly how Earth's interior materials react. But one thing's for sure: the ground beneath your feet would be a much wilder, more unpredictable place.

Imagine this:

Walking home from school, you feel a sudden tremor, a "mini quake." It's not enough to knock you over, but it's enough to make your lunch box rattle.

A new mountain starts sprouting on your favorite hiking trail.

Your science textbook comes with a warning: "Please do not open during volcanic eruptions."

Geology nerds would be thrilled. The rest of us? Maybe not so much.

Life: Could We Survive?

So, we have a planet twice the size, gravity twice as strong, and earthquakes on steroids. What about us—humans? Could we handle this mega-Earth?

Gravity doubling is a massive deal.

Right now, Earth's gravity pulls you down with a force that your body is perfectly adapted to. Your bones have a certain strength to hold you upright, your muscles are toned just right to move you around, and even your blood pumps efficiently against gravity.

But double gravity? That's like suddenly carrying your own weight plus a backpack full of bricks every second of the day. You'd be basically lifting yourself constantly.

Here's what that means:

Bones: To avoid collapsing under their own weight, bones would need to be denser and thicker. Our current skeletons would feel like toothpicks. In fact, early humans on this Earth 2.0 might have evolved with stockier, shorter frames to better support the extra weight.

Muscles: Your muscles would need to generate twice the force for simple actions like walking, standing up, or lifting a pencil. Sports would require serious strength training just to compete.

Cardiovascular system: Your heart would work overtime to pump blood upwards, especially to your brain, fighting that extra gravitational pull.

What about animals?

Flying creatures would struggle big time. Birds and bats rely on lightweight bodies and powerful wings to defy gravity. Doubling gravity would make flying way harder, if not impossible, for many species. Maybe only tiny insects could still flutter around.

On the bright side, land animals might become stronger and more compact. Think rhino-sized squirrels or muscular rabbits.

Plants, too, would feel the squeeze:

Trees would struggle to grow tall. Stronger gravity pulls harder on trunks and branches, so we might see forests of shorter, stockier trees with thick trunks. Imagine a world without the towering redwoods or majestic sequoias.

Plants might invest more energy into strengthening roots and stems rather than growing tall, changing ecosystems entirely.

In short, life would have to adapt to a much heavier, more demanding environment.

Bonus: What About You?

Let's zoom in on you—yes, you—the mega-Earth teenager.

Picture this:

Your school backpack weighs double what it does now. Forget "too heavy to carry"—it's basically your workout routine.

Sports? Sprinting would feel like running through mud. Your muscles scream, and your stamina tanks fast.

Flying drones? Those cute little gadgets that zip around would struggle to lift off in the thicker air and higher gravity.

Climbing a hill feels more like climbing Everest.

Even simple things like jumping onto the bus or hopping off the curb would require superhuman effort.

On the flip side, you get bragging rights:

"Yeah, I live on the biggest planet in the solar system now. No big deal."

Your gym sessions make you a natural superhero.

Maybe you develop super strong legs and arms just from everyday life.

Wrapping It Up: Twice as Big, Twice as Wild

So, doubling Earth's diameter sounds like a neat science experiment, but the reality is a planet transformed. Gravity doubles, making everything heavier and more exhausting.

The atmosphere thickens, changing how we breathe and how the weather behaves. Oceans spread wider and get deeper, with wild tides. Tectonic activity kicks into high gear, shaking the planet more often. Life would evolve (or struggle) to cope with the heavier conditions.

Would humans survive? Probably—with some serious evolutionary upgrades and a lot of strength training. Or maybe we'd all just binge-watch shows and avoid climbing stairs.

Either way, a twice-as-big Earth would be a wild, heavier, more intense place—a planet you'd have to work hard to live on, but one that's fascinating to imagine.

And here's to you for finishing the first 10 chapters of this book.

XI

What If Humans Had Wings?

Let's just get this out of the way first: I've *always* wanted to fly.

Not in a cramped aeroplane next to someone who brings sandwiches for snacks (why do they always sit next to me?), but really fly—soaring above cities, swooping down like a superhero, dodging pigeons mid-air, and maybe even making dramatic landings in math class to delay tests. And so, like every scientifically curious daydreamer, I had one question:

What if humans had wings?

But not just decorative, cosplay-style wings. I'm talking about big, strong, fully functional wings that flap and lift and glide and give you a legit "Sorry I'm late, I flew into a storm over Delhi" excuse.

Let's unfold this idea, feather by feather.

1. The Science of Flight: Can We Even Lift Off?

First things first: physics. I know, I know—science class isn't always the most soaring experience, but bear with me.

Birds fly because their bodies are designed for it. Hollow bones, powerful chest muscles, lightweight bodies, and, most importantly, a large enough wingspan compared to their body weight.

Here's a quick sciencey tidbit: The heaviest bird that can actually fly is the great bustard. It weighs about 15 kg and has a wingspan of 2.4 meters. Now compare that to the average human—say 60–70 kg. That's a lot of extra mass to get off the ground.

To make a human fly like a bird, we'd need wings about 7 to 10 meters wide—that's longer than a school bus. Imagine walking into your classroom with those stuck to your back. Forget chairs—you'd need a parking space.

Also, our bones are dense. Birds have spongy, hollow bones that make them light. If humans were to fly, we'd need to give up milk and grow bird-like bones. But then, we'd risk breaking an arm just by tripping over a Lego.

2. The Evolutionary Angle: Feathered Ancestors?

Let's imagine that, millions of years ago, some quirky branch of primates looked at the sky, watched birds soaring freely, and thought, "You know what? That looks fun." So they started evolving wings. Slowly, over generations, natural selection gave them feathers, lighter frames, and the ability to take to the skies. Fast forward to today—and boom! We, Homo volaticus, are strutting around with wings folded behind our backs.

But for that to work, our bodies would have to be seriously different from what we've got now. Here's what evolution would likely have reshaped:

Massive Pectoral Muscles

You thought bodybuilders had big chests? Nope. If we had functional wings capable of lifting our entire body weight into the air, our pectoralis major muscles (those big chest muscles birds use to flap) would be huge. Like, "ripped eagle" huge. Say goodbye to spaghetti arms and flat chests—everyone would walk around like a jacked gymnast with wings.

Also, imagine gym class. No more push-ups. Now it's 100 flaps a minute or you fail. Protein shakes? More like feather fuel smoothies.

Lightweight Bodies

Human bones are solid and dense—perfect for surviving clumsy accidents and school hallway shoving matches. But flying demands something else: a lighter frame.

Birds evolved pneumatized (hollow) bones to cut down weight without sacrificing strength. So, in our winged version, we'd likely have delicate, air-filled bones. That means no more tackling in football. One wrong move and someone's clavicle crumbles like a breadstick.

Also, our overall body size would shrink. Sorry, tall folks—you'd probably be scaled down to a featherweight flyer. Less mass = more air time.

Redesigning the Spine and Skeletal System

Flapping massive wings attached to your back would need a full skeletal redesign. Our current spine is great for walking upright, dancing awkwardly at weddings, and carrying schoolbags—but it's not great for launching into the sky.

To support wings, we'd need:

A wider, sturdier ribcage to anchor those huge flight muscles.

A keeled sternum, like birds have—a big ridge of bone where flight muscles attach.

Shoulder joints rotated backward, so wings could flap up and down efficiently.

A more horizontal torso orientation. So forget standing tall—we'd probably walk around in a slightly crouched, forward-leaning posture, like ninja chickens.

Basically, evolution would turn us into a mash-up of a gymnast, a bird, and a parkour expert. Not the worst combo.

The Feathery Stuff

Ah yes, the feathers. Not just for looks—feathers are engineering marvels. They're lightweight, strong, flexible, and capable of trapping air for lift and insulation.

But—and this is a big but—they're high maintenance. Birds spend hours preening: cleaning, straightening, oiling, and fluffing their feathers to keep them flight-ready. If we had wings, we'd need to do the same. Which means...

New school rules: "All students must carry a feather comb. No excuses."

Morning routines: Wake up. Brush teeth. Fix feathers. Apply anti-molt spray.

Social judgment: "Ugh, did you see Ananya's feathers today? So frizzy."

And let's not forget molting season. Once a year, your feathers would fall out and grow back. Everyone would look like awkward, half-bald pigeons for weeks. Fashion brands would cash in with "molting cloaks" and "feather fillers."

3. How Society Would Change: Say Goodbye to Traffic

Let's say we *did* evolve with wings. Society would be wildly different.

Transportation: Gone are the days of bumper-to-bumper traffic. People would flap out of their 15th-floor apartments and zip through the air to school or work. No more "stuck in traffic"—only "stuck in a flock."

But air travel would come with its own problems: mid-air collisions, bad weather, and rogue seagulls. (Those guys already act like they own the skies.)

Also, cities would look different. No need for roads. Instead, we'd have sky-lanes and mid-air parking. Tall buildings would have "wing decks" instead of elevators. Drones would become air traffic controllers, constantly yelling "Clear the zone! Incoming grandma at 2 o'clock!"

Shopping and Daily Life: Carrying groceries would be a nightmare. Ever tried flapping with three bags of tomatoes and a watermelon? No thank you.

People might develop little wing-holsters or even hire "wingless" delivery folks who stick to the ground. (In this world, not everyone might evolve wings equally. Classism by wingspan? Oh boy.)

Also, sports would be unrecognizable. Sky-basketball, wing-marathons, aerial wrestling... And forget about hide-and-seek. People would just flap up to a rooftop.

4. Wing Maintenance: Feather Fallouts and Hygiene Nightmares

Wings aren't just plug-and-play. Real wings—like those of birds—require constant upkeep.

Feathers molt. They fall off and regrow. So, every few months, you'd be walking around with one wing half-bald. And people would be like, "Bro, you flying economy today?"

Also, hygiene would be a whole thing. Imagine PE class with sweaty wings. Ew. There'd be special deodorizers, wing sprays, and maybe even salons just for feathers: "Feather & Shine – Where Your Wings Take Flight!"

Wing lice might become a thing. And people might judge others like, "Did you see his feathers? So oily."

5. The Environmental Impact: Beware the Bird Poop Apocalypse

Birds poop mid-air. That's a fact. If we had wings, and if our digestive systems followed bird logic (which we hope it wouldn't), the sky would be a dangerous place.

Umbrellas would be a necessity, even on sunny days. Buildings might install "splat shields." And you'd probably need a "sky bathroom etiquette" law enforced by aerial cops.

Also, more humans in the air means less reliance on cars—yay for reduced pollution! But it might mean more accidents, bird-human collisions, and the need for constant weather updates.

6. Predator Problems: Hello, Sky Predators!

If we lived in the skies, we wouldn't be alone. Nature would adapt too.

Birds of prey like eagles and falcons would suddenly see us as competition. Imagine having to outfly a golden eagle just to get to school. Hawk attacks during exams? Suddenly, "I was attacked by an eagle" becomes a legit excuse.

There might even be sky territories, with certain gangs or flocks dominating airspace. (Yes, I know I'm describing Angry Birds: Human Edition.)

7. Would Everyone Have Wings?

That's a tough one. In most bird species, everyone has wings, but not all fly equally well. Penguins have wings but can't fly. Chickens kind of fly, but only if they really, really believe in themselves.

So maybe in our human-winged world, there'd be all kinds:

The gliders – people who use wings like a parachute, mostly floating down from buildings.

The sprinters – short-distance flyers, like human hummingbirds.

The aerobats – doing flips and loops for fun (or TikTok).

The grounded – some humans might have tiny wings, just for decoration. Think fancy shoulder blades with feathers.

This would lead to all sorts of new social categories and competitions: "National Flap-Off 2025," "Longest Hover," and "Best Feather Colour Coordination."

8. Fashion and Function

Let's be honest, fashion would be fabulous. Wings come in all kinds of colours, shapes, and fluffiness levels. You could dye your feathers, add glitter, or braid them into your hair.

Clothing would adapt, of course. No more backpacks. No tight jackets. Wing-holes would be standard. Maybe even capes for protection (a cape over wings—how ironic).

And of course, online stores would sell everything from feather straighteners to monsoon-proof wing covers. (Imagine trying to fly in the rain—slippery feathers are not aerodynamic.)

9. *The Emotional Side: Mental Health and Freedom*

Now here's the deeper part. Flying gives a sense of freedom. Birds don't just fly to get places—they soar. It looks like joy. If we had wings, maybe humans would spend more time in nature. Looking down from the sky might change how we think about the Earth, pollution, or even war.

Sky gazing would be replaced by sky joining. Clouds wouldn't be distant—they'd be part of your morning commute.

Flying could even become a form of therapy. "Feeling stressed? Take a lap around the stratosphere." (Though make sure you check the weather app. Flying into a thundercloud isn't very relaxing.)

10. *But... Would It Be Worth It?*

So after all this flapping about, here's the real question: Would having wings actually make life better?

Maybe.

Flying would be incredible. It would change everything—from cities to schools to how we think about freedom. But it would also come with serious complications. Biology, society, fashion, and safety would all have to evolve together.

Still... when I look at birds gliding peacefully across the sky, a part of me whispers:

"What if...?"

And I smile, knowing that even if humans never grow wings, we'll always have imagination—and maybe a hang glider.

Final Thought:

If humans had wings, our bodies would change, our society would transform, and the sky would become our playground. But until evolution catches up (or someone invents super-powered jet feathers), I guess we'll just keep dreaming.

Or maybe... take paragliding lessons?

Just in case.

XII

What If The Sun Blinked Off For 24 Hours?

It's a beautiful morning. You wake up, stretch, and pull your curtains aside. Something's off. Really off.

No sunlight.

No glowing horizon.

Just stars. Everywhere.

It's 8 AM and it looks like midnight.

No, you didn't sleep through the apocalypse. The Sun has—wait for it—blinked. Just like a big cosmic eye, our giant star decided to shut off for 24 hours. No explosions. No warnings. Just click—darkness.

Now, obviously, the Sun doesn't have eyelids or a light switch. But let's suspend disbelief for a bit and ask: What if the Sun actually did turn off for exactly 24 hours, then turned back on like nothing happened?

Let's break it down—by time, science, and panic levels.

Minute Zero: The Blink Begins

Here's the first weird thing: nobody on Earth notices—at first.

Why?

Because light from the Sun takes about 8 minutes and 20 seconds to reach us. That means when the Sun blinks off, we're still basking in sunlight that left the Sun over eight minutes ago. So, even though the Sun has gone dark, Earth continues glowing for a few minutes like nothing happened.

It's like a horror movie where the power's already out, but you don't realize it until the hallway gets suspiciously quiet.

Minute 9: Lights Out, Panic On

Suddenly, everything changes.

Across the globe, skies darken instantly. One second it's bright daylight, and the next—it's space. Stars are visible even in big cities. Planes have to switch to emergency lighting. Solar panels stop working. Photosynthesis hits pause. Streetlights pop on. Phones buzz with emergency alerts.

Twitter explodes. Memes flood Instagram:

"Sun's taking a day off. Mood."

Conspiracy theories bloom like mushrooms:

"Aliens stole our star."

"Global blackout—solar version."

"NASA is hiding the second sun!"

Meanwhile, scientists are freaking out in a more useful way.

The Science: What Just Happened?

Here's the impossible scenario we're pretending is real:

The Sun doesn't explode (because if it did, we'd all be toast). It doesn't go cold permanently (which would slowly kill all life). It just... stops emitting light and energy for 24 hours.

Like someone hit a giant cosmic pause button.

No sunlight. No solar wind. No UV rays. No heat.

Just darkness.

This is physically impossible under known science (unless you've got magic, aliens, or a bored universe-simulator), but we're running with it.

So what actually happens during those 24 hours?

Hour 1–3: The Big Chill Begins

Without sunlight, Earth starts to cool down. Fast.

But here's the interesting part: it doesn't become instant ice age. The atmosphere, oceans, and landmass store heat. So the drop is gradual—at first. In the first few hours, temperatures dip by a few degrees. Cities feel like late twilight on a chilly evening. People assume it's an eclipse. A very, very weird one.

But scientists quickly confirm: "Yeah, the Sun is gone. Temporarily, we hope."

By Hour 3, crop fields are shutting down photosynthesis. Animals are confused. Bees are bumping into things. Birds are landing early. Bats are having a party.

Hour 6–12: Earth Becomes a Fridge

By now, temperatures are on a rollercoaster whooping down. Global average temp may drop by 10–15°C (18–27°F) or more. Deserts cool fastest—no clouds, no mercy. Tropical areas dip into sweater weather. Polar regions? Absolute deep-freeze.

And remember: no solar power. Entire countries relying on solar grids? They're in the dark—literally. Backup generators fire up. Energy conservation becomes a trending hashtag.

Meanwhile:

Plants are basically asleep.

Humans are layering up and charging flashlights.

Farmers are praying for photosynthesis to come back.

And pets? Pets are just excited you're home early.

Night Side Chaos

Remember, half the planet was already in night when this happened. For them, it's now the longest night in history. And it gets creepy. No sunrise at 6 AM. No change in the sky at all.

Just... more stars. And fear.

Crime rates may spike due to extended darkness. Anxiety skyrockets. Some people throw end-of-the-world parties. Others start building indoor farms.

The only upside? The sky is gorgeous. With no sunlight scattering through the atmosphere, the stars are clearer than ever. The Milky Way looks like someone spilled glitter across the universe.

Astronomers are thrilled. Everyone else? Not so much.

Hour 13–20: Serious Cooling Mode

By now, Earth is shivering. Global average temperatures may have dropped 20°C (36°F) or more. Some places are experiencing sub-zero temperatures that have never seen snow before. Ocean surfaces begin to cool. Atmospheric circulation slows. Weather patterns start acting weird. Fog rolls in over cities. Cold winds whip through tropical towns.

Most worrying of all? Power grids are overwhelmed. People without heating are in danger. Wildlife starts dying. Crops begin irreversible damage.

Scientists urge calm and focus on essentials:

Keep warm.

Conserve power.

Eat shelf-stable food.

Theories about why this is happening range from scientific (massive solar anomaly!) to bizarre (the Sun's taking a nap?).

Alien Theories and Human Emotions

People cope in weird ways.

Some think aliens have covered the Sun with a sphere. Others believe it's divine punishment for too many reels and boring stuff. A few cults start gathering in fields, expecting resurrection or new light.

But for most people, it's simple:

They miss the warmth. They miss the light. They miss the Sunrise.

We don't realize how deeply we rely on the Sun—not just for life, but for hope.

Hour 24: Light Returns

And then—just like that—it's back.

At exactly the 24-hour mark, the Sun blinks on.

Instantly, light floods the planet. Shadows snap back. Temperatures begin to rise. Solar panels hum again. Birds start chirping in confusion. Photosynthesis kicks back in. Crops begin their green magic.

The world breathes a collective sigh of relief. It's over.

People step outside and stare upward, grateful, blinking like cave dwellers seeing light for the first time.

So What Would Actually Happen?

Let's science it up:

No permanent damage to Earth's orbit or tilt—the Sun's gravity never stopped.

No mass extinction—just disruption. If it had lasted longer than a few days, that'd be different.

Crops and ecosystems would recover—though some sensitive species might suffer.

Massive economic losses—especially for agriculture and solar-reliant energy grids.

New appreciation for the Sun—and probably a lot of sun-themed art.

In short: it'd be a bizarre, terrifying, chilly day—but survivable. Just barely.

Final Thought: The 24-Hour Reset

This cosmic power outage would teach humanity a few things:

We depend on the Sun for everything.

Our planet is resilient—but not invincible.

And when the lights go out, we rediscover what really matters: warmth, food, light, and... each other.

Also, you can bet every country would invest in Sun Blink Contingency Plans going forward. Heat banks, artificial grow lights, emergency thermal gear, and about 100 documentaries with titles like "The Day the Sun Went Out."

So, the next time you walk outside and feel the sunlight on your face, don't take it for granted. Because somewhere out there, in some strange alternate universe, Earth might still be waiting for the blink to end.

XIII

What If Aliens Are Watching Us Like A Reality Show?

Imagine you're an alien.

No, not the green slimy kind with antennae and a catchphrase like "Take me to your leader." Let's say you're a highly evolved being with twelve sensory organs, a head shaped like an organic Bluetooth speaker, and the ability to see across 87 dimensions (but still get bored on Sundays).

Now imagine you're sitting in your cosmic recliner, somewhere in Galaxy QZ-17, munching on salted asteroid chips, flipping through your version of Netflix—let's call it ExoStream—when you land on your favorite pleasure:

"Earth: The Reality Show."

Yes, humans. Us. You. Me. All of us. We are the stars of a planet-sized show, being secretly watched by alien audiences light-years away.

Ridiculous? Maybe. Entertaining? Absolutely. Impossible? Well, let's talk.

Part 1: Why Would Aliens Even Care?

Let's get one thing straight—Earth is weird.

To aliens, we're that messy drama-filled planet that can't stop fighting with itself, builds skyscrapers and nukes in the same decade, and keeps arguing about pineapple on pizza.

We:

- Poison our own air, then sell bottled clean air.
- Invented nuclear weapons and duck face selfies within 50 years.
- Send billion-dollar probes into space, but lose TV remotes in couch cushions for eternity.
- Are the only known species to create inflatable flamingo pool floats and also particle accelerators.

In short: we're endlessly entertaining.

To aliens, Earth might be the ultimate soap opera. High drama. Strange rituals. Sudden plot twists (Like those TV shows, where the family can't stop crying after their kid leaves the home). Occasional scientific breakthroughs. And always—always—some politician doing something ridiculous.

Part 2: But Seriously, Could Aliens Watch Us?

Let's get nerdy.

There are actually some scientific theories and speculations—admittedly fringe, but not completely outlandish—that suggest if advanced extraterrestrial civilizations exist, they might be observing us from afar. Not out of malice or curiosity, but for the same reason we watch nature documentaries: to understand behavior, evolution, and maybe... entertainment?

One of the most fascinating ideas is a real scientific concept called the Zoo Hypothesis.

Coined by MIT radio astronomer John Ball in 1973, the hypothesis suggests that alien civilizations know we're here—but are intentionally keeping their distance. Like zookeepers who don't want to interfere with the animals in their care, they avoid contact to let us develop naturally. No spoilers. No alien cameos. Just silent observation.

They're watching. Studying. Recording. Maybe rating our seasons and shipping characters like we do on our favorite shows.

And possibly—laughing at our Wi-Fi problems, pineapple-on-pizza debates, and inability to walk through revolving doors gracefully.

But how could they actually pull this off?

Part 3: The Tech of Alien Reality TV

If aliens are observing us, they'd need surveillance tools. Let's break down the possibilities:

1. Quantum Telescopes

Way beyond our Hubble or James Webb, these would let aliens see Earth in real-time—even across light-years. It's like Zoom, but with zero lag and infinite resolution. Bad news if you were dancing in your room yesterday. Good news if you want to be famous across galaxies.

2. Nanobot Observers

Tiny, invisible bots seeded into Earth's atmosphere thousands of years ago. They float, fly, or cling to surfaces. Some live in your microwave. One might be in your left sock. They record everything. Including your 3 AM fridge raids.

3. Gravitational Recorders

Aliens who mastered the manipulation of gravity waves might use them to detect even the smallest changes on Earth—conversations, actions, probably your heartbeat when you see your crush.

4. TV Signal Time Travel

For decades, Earth's radio and TV signals have been beaming into space. "I Love Lucy," moon landings, cricket matches, and cat videos—they've all shot out into the cosmos. If aliens are sitting 50 light-years away, they're watching reruns of the 1970s right now.

And yes—possibly judging our fashion choices.

Part 4: Earth's Greatest Hits (According to Alien Viewers)

If you were an alien TV critic, Earth would have peak moments.

Here's a probable highlight reel:

1. Season 4,000 BCE: Humans invent the wheel. (First product placement opportunity!)
2. Season 44 CE: Romans go full drama. Lots of togas. 4.5 stars.
3. Season 1492: Big plot twist—worlds collide. Viewers shocked.

4. Season 1969: Man lands on moon. Everyone cheers. Aliens laugh because they've got lunar food courts.
5. Season 2020: Global pandemic. Emotional arc. Record-breaking viewership.
6. Season 2023: People put cheese on coffee. Aliens threaten to cancel the show.

And let's not forget the side-plots: the Cold War, Area 51 memes, cricket vs baseball debates, dog influencers, Flat Earth resurgence (a fan-favourite subplot in the "irony" genre), and billions of individual human lives—all part of the grand narrative.

Part 5: Do We Get Votes?

If Earth is a reality show, do we have any agency? Are aliens just watching? Or are they... meddling?

Maybe every once in a while, they vote on plot twists.

"Should we let them invent electricity? Press Y/N."

"Drop a meteor or see how this internet thing goes?"

"Interfere with pyramids? Bonus points for mystery."

"Release a new virus? Nah, too soon."

Maybe the reason some events feel so scripted—like a certain billionaire naming his child after a math equation—is because they were literally chosen by viewers across the galaxy.

Which also means...maybe you were a fan favorite once. That moment when you said something unexpectedly brilliant or stood up for someone else? A camera might've zoomed in.

Part 6: Are the Ratings Dropping?

Let's be honest—recent seasons have been a mess.

War. Pollution. Doomscrolling. Conspiracy theories. Climate change. Reboots of movies that didn't need reboots. If aliens are still watching, they might be debating whether to:

Renew the show

Intervene to spice up the drama

Or cancel Earth altogether

In fact, maybe the asteroid that wiped out the dinosaurs was a "mid-season reset." And we're the reboot. You know, "Earth: The Human Chapter." If that's true, we'd better step it up. Or worse, we might get replaced by the next spinoff:

"Mars Colonists: Red Dust Diaries."

Part 7: What If We Find Out?

Now the biggest twist of all: What happens if one day we find out it's all true? A whistleblowing alien sends us the link to Earth's channel. We watch our lives on interstellar DVR. Every decision. Every dance. Every bad haircut.

How would that change us?

Would we:

Try to impress the alien audience?

Live more ethically, knowing we're being watched?

Burn our phones and hide in forests?

Demand royalties?

And if we knew we were watched... would we become better?

Final Scene: Lights, Camera, Humanity

So here we are, under invisible spotlights, starring in a show we never auditioned for. Are aliens watching? Who knows. Is it funny to imagine? Absolutely.

But whether or not they're tuning in, someone always is:

The people around us.

The generations after us.

Ourselves, in moments of reflection.

So maybe we should live like we're on camera. Not to impress... but to be real.

Because the best stories? They're not the perfect ones.

They're the ones where characters grow, connect, mess up, learn, and keep going anyway.

So go ahead—dance badly. Dream big. Be kind. Fail loudly.

The universe might just be watching. And rooting for you.

XIV

What If Your Dreams Were Real In Another Dimension?

"I just had the weirdest dream last night."

That's how it always starts, right? One minute you're a normal teenager stressing over math homework, and the next, you're flying a unicorn into a space-doughnut battle against ninjas. Totally normal. But have you ever wondered—what if that wasn't just your imagination? What if that dream actually happened... in another dimension?

Welcome to the multiverse, where your dreams might not be just dreams. They might be alternate realities playing out while you drool on your pillow.

Sounds like science fiction? Great. Because this chapter is full of it. And also full of science. Strap in, because we're about to cross the boundary between sleep and quantum theory—with a side of brain juice and cosmic delicacies.

The Multiverse Café: A Brief Introduction

Imagine a café. But instead of people sipping overpriced coffee, each table is a different universe. One where dinosaurs never went extinct. One where cats are in charge of governments. One where your parents never met, and poof, no you.

This is the multiverse—short for "multiple universes." A theoretical concept supported by some branches of physics, especially quantum mechanics and string theory. The idea is that every decision, every possibility, splits reality like a cosmic "Choose Your Own Adventure" book. You chose toast instead of cereal this morning? Congrats, there's now a dimension where you're currently crunching on cornflakes. Exciting.

Now, here's where it gets juicy.

Some physicists, like Hugh Everett (who came up with the Many Worlds Interpretation), believe that every quantum event creates a branching universe. So, while you're dreaming of becoming a godly astronaut with a superpower, in another dimension, that exact scenario might actually be playing out. Seriously.

The Science of Dreams

Before we get too deep into interdimensional hopping, let's rewind and look at how dreams even work. Dreams mostly happen during REM (Rapid Eye Movement) sleep. That's the stage where your brain lights up like a disco ball, especially in areas linked to memory, emotion, and imagination.

Scientists used to think dreams were just random firings of neurons—a nightly brain fart, essentially. But more recent studies show they serve a purpose. Dreaming helps process emotions, solve problems, rehearse scenarios (like punching your math teacher, but, uh, don't actually do that), and strengthen memory connections.

Basically, your brain becomes a weird theater director, mixing reality, memory, imagination, and that one time you saw a dancing tree on YouTube into a dream-movie. The result? You, desperately finding that tree and maybe as well start dancing with it. Classic.

But what if this nightly production isn't just entertainment?

Quantum Entanglement and Dream Dial-Up

Here's where we connect the dots between science and sci-fi.

Quantum entanglement is a phenomenon where two particles, even light years apart, are mysteriously connected. You change one, the other changes instantly. Spooky, right? Even Einstein called it "spooky action at a distance."

Now imagine this: what if your brain, during dreaming, is somehow entangled with a version of you in a parallel universe? Not physically, but on a quantum level. Possible, right?

Think of it like an interdimensional dial-up connection (kids, ask your parents about the old dialups). You fall asleep, your brain tunes into the frequency of a "you" in another universe, and boom—you're seeing their life. Their adventures. Their weird obsession with things you hate.

This might explain why dreams often feel real. Because, in a way, they are. Just not here.

Meet Dream You: A Multiverse Travelogue

Let's meet some offs, shall we?

Dream You #1: Commander Kaul of Mars Base Alpha

In Universe 287X-Gamma, you're the youngest space commander on Mars. You've domesticated Martian hamsters (they bark), solved interdimensional Sudoku, and invented edible space socks.

Dream You #2: Lizard Monarch of Reptilia-5

Here, evolution went the other way. You're a sentient lizard in a cape, ruling a swampy empire. Your chief advisor is a talking frog named Sir Hopsalot, and your biggest threat is the annual invasion of iguanas.

Dream You #3: Regular You, But With a Beard

Exactly like this universe, except you have a beard. Even if you're twelve. Especially if you're twelve. Don't question it.

These alternate "yous" may feel like figments of your imagination, but what if they're memories—echoes—picked up by your dreaming brain from another dimension?

Woah...now it's getting interesting.

Brain as a Cosmic Receiver

Now you might ask, "How can my squishy pink brain pick up signals from another universe?"

Great question. Scientists have found that the human brain gives off electromagnetic signals, and some speculate that consciousness could be tied to quantum processes. This is fringe science, but intriguing.

A 2020 paper in Frontiers in Psychology explored the idea of "quantum consciousness"—where consciousness arises from quantum vibrations inside brain neurons. British physicist Sir Roger Penrose even suggested that microtubules in brain cells might be involved in quantum computations.

Basically, your brain might not just be a hunk of neurons. It might be a hyper-advanced quantum processor capable of tuning into multiple dimensions—especially during the wild, rule-free chaos of REM sleep.

Which brings us to the real question...

Are You the Dream, or the Dreamer?

Here's a philosophical curveball: What if the "you" reading this is the dream, and the one in your dreams is the real deal?

Think about it. In dreams, time feels stretchy. Logic is fuzzy. Gravity sometimes takes a vacation. But you feel like you (without actually looking at you). There's emotion, decision-making, even memory (sometimes of things you've never done here).

So, what defines "real"? Is it consistency? Sensory input? Memory?

There's a theory called "Simulation Hypothesis" proposed by philosopher Nick Bostrom. It suggests that we might be living in a simulated reality. So maybe our waking life is just another level of the multiverse—and the dreams? Windows into base reality.

Whoa.

Let's take a brain break. Eat a cookie. Hug your dog. Okay, let's continue.

The Psychology of Dream Dimensions

From Freud to Jung to modern neuroscientists, everyone's tried to decode dreams. Freud said they were wish fulfillment. Jung thought they were the language of the unconscious.

But let's go deeper.

In 2004, neuroscientist J. Allan Hobson proposed that dreams are the brain's way of making sense of random neural activity. But what if that "random" activity is actually data from other versions of you? Psychologists studying lucid dreaming—a state where the dreamer knows they're dreaming—have shown that the brain can be trained to take control in dreams. Lucid dreamers can fly, manipulate time, even interview their dream characters.

If dreams were just random fluff, how could you control them? What if lucid dreaming is you taking the wheel of another "you's" life for a night? Like a cosmic timeshare.

Scientifically Speaking: Can We Test This?

Let's say you want to test this idea. Can we prove our dreams are windows to alternate dimensions?

Sadly, we can't (yet). But science is trying.

Neural Mapping of Dreams: Scientists in Japan have used fMRI scans to map brain activity during dreams and predict visual imagery. One day, this tech might let us record dreams—dream Netflix, anyone?

Quantum Brain Hypothesis: If future studies show evidence of quantum entanglement in neurons, it could support the idea that our brains are capable of interdimensional processing.

Shared Dreaming Experiments: Some fringe studies have explored "mutual dreaming" where two people dream similar things on the same night. Results are inconsistent, but the idea is fascinating.

Dangers of Dream-Hopping

Okay, but let's say you really can access other dimensions in your sleep. Sounds fun, right?

Well... maybe not always.

What if Dream You has enemies? Interdimensional tax collectors? Ninja ducks? What if you get trapped in a dream-world, Inception-style? There's even a real disorder called REM Sleep Behavior Disorder (RBD) where people physically act out dreams. Imagine waking up mid-fencing match with your lamp.

So maybe it's for the best that the portal closes when we wake up. For now.

So... What Now?

The next time you wake up after a bizarre dream, don't dismiss it. Maybe it wasn't nonsense. Maybe you were busy saving penguins from a chocolate tsunami on Planet Snax-12. And maybe, just maybe, the penguins are real—and they miss you.

Dreams are weird, yes. But they might be the universe's way of letting us peek behind the curtain. Into a vast, complex multiverse. Into the lives we could have had—or still do have—somewhere out there.

So go ahead. Nap like a hero. And remember:

You're not just sleeping.

You're travelling.

PS: "If you ever find yourself eating spaghetti with a walrus in your dream, be kind. In his dimension, you're the weird one."

XV

What If The Speed Of Light Was 100x Slower?

Hey sloths! Looks like your dream just came true. Well...kind sloths, would you mind thinking about us, the main – with brain – creatures on this land too?

Let's Begin with a Speed Limit

There's a cosmic speed limit—and it's not your Wi-Fi at your house. It's the speed of light: 299,792,458 meters per second. That's around 300,000 kilometres per second. Or if you prefer more relatable units, light can circle the Earth 7.5 times in a single second.

That's fast. Like, "Catch me if you can, good luck!" fast.

But... what if we slowed that bad boy down?

Let's say—just for the giggles of cosmic curiosity—that the speed of light was 100 times slower.

So instead of 300,000 km/s, light would crawl along at 3,000 km/s. That's just a little bit faster than a hypersonic jet. Still quick, but in universal terms? That's glacial.

It sounds harmless, right? But hold onto your photons, because everything—and I mean everything—would change. From how we age to how stars burn to whether we'd even exist.

First Things First: You Would See Nothing… Literally

First, let's talk visibility. Light takes about 8 minutes and 20 seconds to reach Earth from the Sun. If light were 100x slower, it would take:

8 minutes x 100 = 800 minutes = 13 hours and 20 minutes

So you'd wake up in the morning and look outside to… darkness. Because the light from the Sun is still making its way over. Sunrise would be on a 13-hour delay. You'd literally be seeing yesterday's Sun.

Stars? Forget it. The nearest star to us (Proxima Centauri) is already 4.24 light-years away. With slowed light, that's 424 years away. So the night sky wouldn't sparkle like it does now. Most stars would be invisible, their photons crawling through the dark like arthritic snails.

We'd basically live in a time-delayed universe—like watching everything on a broken livestream.

Time Travel, But Not the Cool Kind

In our real universe, nothing can move faster than light, which is why light acts like the ultimate universal boundary line between "now" and "later."

If we slow light down, you might think: "Hey, doesn't that make time travel easier?"

Not quite.

Because everything else would change too. Slower light means that relativity—Einstein's baby—would get a complete cosmic wedgie. Time dilation, GPS calculations, even cause-and-effect logic would break down.

Let's say you turned on a flashlight to help your friend cross a dark cave. Normally, they'd see it instantly (ish). But now, the light takes so long to reach them, they could trip over a rock and sue you for negligence before your beam gets there.

Moral of the story: Time is linked with the speed of light. Slowing light makes "now" and "later" incredibly fuzzy. That's not time travel. That's just pure chaos.

Gravity Goes Nuts (Thanks a Lot, Einstein)

According to Einstein's theory of general relativity, gravity is not just a force—it's the curvature of space-time. And gravitational effects also travel at the speed of light.

If light slows down, so does gravity.

Let that sink in: You could suddenly shift the Sun, and we wouldn't feel the gravitational consequences for over 13 hours. Earth's orbit would be out of sync with solar movement, causing potential orbital havoc. Planets might veer off-course. Moons might drift away. Celestial ballet becomes interplanetary bumper cars.

Also, we wouldn't feel gravity slower in day-to-day terms (like you wouldn't float off your chair), but changes in gravity would lag dramatically. It's like texting the universe and waiting 13 hours for the blue ticks.

Technology Says Goodbye

Let's talk internet.

Fiber optics—those sleek glass tubes that shoot pulses of light to deliver Shorts to your phone—rely on light speed. If that speed is reduced to a 100th, your 2-second video buffer time becomes a 3-minute tea break. Streaming Netflix? Might as well dust off your DVD collection.

Microwave ovens? Dead. They rely on electromagnetic radiation moving at light speed. A 30-second popcorn session now takes 50 minutes. Try explaining that to your stomach at midnight. GPS? Also ruined. GPS satellites depend on the timing of light-speed signals to tell you where you are. Slowed light throws off your location by kilometers. You ask for directions to the café, and your phone drops you in the Pacific Ocean.

In short: welcome to the Great Technological Blackout.

Chemistry and Photosynthesis… Broken

Photosynthesis—the reason we have oxygen, food, and that one kid in class obsessed with growing mint in a jar—relies on sunlight. If sunlight takes 13 hours to arrive, and is weaker because the photons are strung out in slow-mo, then plants are basically starving all the time. Trees grow slower. Crops underperform. The world becomes a salad-free wasteland.

Even at the atomic level, things fall apart. The electromagnetic force (which holds atoms and molecules together) is mediated by photons—the same particles that make up light.

If photons are sluggish, then chemical reactions—like burning, digestion, or anything remotely life-related—slow down to near-zero.

Lighting a match could take an hour.

Digesting pizza? Try a week.

Your brain signals? Like typing with a rusty spoon.

Basically: biology as we know it collapses.

Stars Wouldn't Shine

Stars—including our own lovable, slightly dramatic fusion ball, the Sun—are basically nuclear power plants in space. At their core, hydrogen atoms smash together under immense pressure and temperature, fusing into helium and releasing enormous amounts of energy in the form of gamma-ray photons.

But here's the twist: those photons don't just zoom out of the star like excited puppies. No—thanks to the dense plasma layers within the star, photons take an excruciatingly long journey to escape. They bump into particles, get absorbed and re-emitted, ricochet like drunk pinballs—over and over again. On average, a photon takes thousands to millions of years to travel from the Sun's core to its surface.

That's already slow. Now imagine the speed of light is 100x slower. The photon's journey becomes 100 times more ridiculous. So instead of a million years to reach the surface, it might take 100 million years. That's more time than it took for the dinosaurs to go from apex predators to museum exhibits.

Here's what this means in practice:

Heat builds up inside the core because the energy has nowhere to go.

Thermal pressure increases dramatically.

The delicate balance between the inward pull of gravity and the outward push of radiation gets thrown off like a toddler on a seesaw with a hippo.

In a normal star, this balance—called hydrostatic equilibrium—keeps things stable. But with energy trapped inside, the outward push weakens. Gravity wins. The star might collapse early or go supernova before it ever has a chance to settle down and become a nice warm ball in the sky.

And what about small stars? They might never ignite at all. Without enough outward radiation pressure to counteract gravitational collapse, they'd just crumple into failed stars—brown dwarfs, gas giants, or worse, massive cosmic lumps of wasted potential. Like the universe ordered a galaxy's worth of IKEA lamps and forgot the bulbs.

The consequences ripple across space:

- No sunlight = no photosynthesis = no plants = no oxygen = no you.
- No starlight = no illumination in the universe = perpetual darkness.
- No stellar life cycles = no supernovae = no heavy elements = no gold, iron, or carbon = no planets, no water, no life, no memes.

Even galaxies would look different. Right now, we see them as stunning spirals and glittering blobs of stars. But in a slow-light universe, they'd be ghostly, dim, barely glowing husks. The Milky Way would look like a sad smear of lint in the sky.

In short, if light is too slow, stars can't release their energy efficiently. Instead of being radiant engines of cosmic creativity, they become bloated heat traps, failed furnaces, or ticking time bombs. The universe wouldn't just be dark and cold—it'd be kind of a cosmic flop, like a galaxy-wide party where nobody remembered to bring electricity.

So, yes, slowing light means stars wouldn't shine—but that's just the start. It would turn the universe into a sad, smoky storage room full of glowing wannabes and stellar underachievers.

You want starlight? Keep those photons fast.

The Upside? Superpowers (Kind of)

Okay, okay. Let's find one silver lining.

If the speed of light were drastically slower—but somehow biology and chemistry still functioned (suspend disbelief, we're in sci-fi now)—some cool stuff could happen.

1. Laser swords would be visible:

In our universe, a laser beam is pretty much invisible from the side. But with slow light, the beam would trail visibly behind like a glowing rope. So real-life lightsabers? Possible. Dangerous. Awesome.

2. High-speed photography in real-time:

Want to watch a bullet in flight? Easy. If light moves slowly, you could see events unfold in cinematic slo-mo in real time. Nature documentaries would be epic.

3. You could dodge lasers.

Finally, all that dodgeball training pays off. Since light-based weapons would move at only 3,000 km/s, you might be able to jump out of the way if you saw it coming far enough in advance. (Spoiler: you won't.)

Cosmic Scale Cancellations

Finally, let's scale up.

The size of the observable universe depends on how far light has traveled since the Big Bang—about 13.8 billion years' worth. With slowed light, the observable universe shrinks 100x smaller. That's only 138 million light-years across—a tiny bubble of cosmic awareness.

Galaxies beyond that? Still there, but we'll never know. Light from them hasn't reached us yet. And never will, not in our lifetimes. Not in a trillion lifetimes. In a slowed-light universe, we become cosmically claustrophobic—a lonely, quiet civilization trapped in a light-deprived cage, staring at the same stars for eternity.

Final Thoughts: A Slower Universe Is a Stranger Universe

If you've ever wished the world would slow down, maybe don't mess with the speed of light.

Because slowing it by even a factor of 100 would:

Make the Sun rise 13 hours late

Erase most stars from the sky

Destroy tech, chemistry, and biology

Break GPS and communication

Cause stars to flicker and die (or not ignite)

Collapse the observable universe into a tiny bubble

Turn cause and effect into a confusing mess

In short: the universe is fine as it is. Light is fast for a reason.

So the next time you switch on a flashlight and instantly see the glow—give a little salute to those speedy photons. They're holding your entire existence together.

And who knew that the tiniest tick of nature's speedometer could decide so much?

XVI

What If Humans Evolved To Live 300 Years?

Let's start with a little thought experiment. Imagine it's your 120th birthday. You're sitting in your garden, surrounded by balloons that say "Just Getting Started," and your great-great-grandkids are running around trying to convince you to finally upgrade your hover-bike. You sigh, sip your algae-protein smoothie, and think, "Wow, only a third of my life is done!"

Sounds wild? Well, welcome to the world where humans live for 300 years.

Now, before we dive into how mind-blowingly awesome—or complicated—that could be, let's put on our science hats and ask: Could this actually happen? And if so, what would that world look like?

The Biology of Living Longer

First things first. Why don't humans already live to 300? The short answer: biology has other plans.

Your body is made up of trillions of cells, and every time a cell divides, a teeny-tiny bit of its DNA called a telomere gets shorter. Think of telomeres like those plastic tips on shoelaces—they protect your chromosomes. But after around 50 divisions (called the Hayflick limit), the cell gets tired and either dies or goes rogue (sometimes becoming cancerous). This is one reason we age.

To live 300 years, we'd need to seriously upgrade our telomere-maintenance system. There's an enzyme called telomerase that can keep telomeres long and happy, but in humans, it's usually only active in certain cells like stem cells. If evolution somehow made telomerase active throughout our bodies without triggering runaway cancer growth... we might be onto something.

Also, our mitochondria—the tiny power plants in our cells—accumulate damage over time from things called free radicals. These are like molecular punks that go around vandalizing our cells. If evolution built better repair mechanisms or antioxidant systems into our biology, we could slow this internal damage.

Bonus idea: what if we evolved like certain animals do? For instance, the naked mole rat lives much longer than expected for its size and seems practically immune to cancer. Meanwhile, greenland sharks can live for over 400 years and still swim chill. Evolution might borrow a few tricks from them.

A 300-Year Brain: Genius or Overload?

Let's say your body is now a finely tuned, age-defying machine. Cool. Wrinkles are minimal, joints work like a dream, and your organs are humming like well-oiled bio-engines. But here's the real question: What about your brain?

Your brain is an incredible piece of wetware, made up of around 86 billion neurons connected through trillions of synapses. Every experience, every piece of knowledge, every embarrassing moment you wish you could forget—it's all stored somewhere in there. But here's the catch: memory isn't infinite.

Think of your brain as a giant, messy hard drive. Over time, files get corrupted, mixed up, or misplaced. Scientists call this cognitive decline. Even in a regular 80-year life, people experience memory fog, slower processing, and the occasional "Why did I walk into this room?" moment. Multiply that by nearly four centuries, and you might just find yourself asking, "Wait... did I invent the anti-gravity engine, or was that my cousin?"

To keep up with a 300-year lifespan, our brains would need an upgrade. Evolution might enhance our hippocampus (the part that processes memory) with higher neuroplasticity and more efficient long-term storage. Instead of forgetting your childhood address, your brain could reorganize memories, file them in categories, and access them like a super-advanced search engine. Think Google, but for your life: "Show me my third birthday party" or "Recall all emotional lessons from past breakups."

And while we're at it, let's talk about emotions over centuries.

Grief. Joy. Awe. These feelings evolve with age even in an 80-year lifespan. So what happens when you're nursing a broken heart... from 112 years ago? Does it become a dull ache? Or does your brain learn to compartmentalize pain better over time? Maybe you start referring to heartbreaks like historical events.

Nostalgia might be deeper, too. Imagine the emotional weight of remembering the smell of fresh paper books from the early 2100s in a future filled with holographic libraries. That old song from your teenage years? It's now a 200-year-old classic—possibly studied in musicology courses.

And let's not forget knowledge accumulation. Assuming your brain can keep learning without hitting a storage cap (thanks, upgraded synapses!), the average 180-year-old might casually drop facts about quantum entanglement, ancient TikTok trends, and Martian geology—in the same conversation. You could hold doctorates in neuroscience, philosophy, architecture, and underwater welding, and still be taking night classes just to "stay sharp."

Also, imagine how this changes creativity. You could develop an entirely new artistic style, master forgotten instruments, write a 20,000-page novel across 50 years, or even invent a whole new genre of entertainment. An evolved brain might not just store more—it might think differently. Faster processing speeds, stronger pattern recognition, deeper emotional insight. Possibly even new forms of intelligence we can't comprehend yet.

But would all of this come at a cost?

Maybe brains would need mental offloading. Picture scheduled "neuro-cleanses," like spring cleaning for your synapses. Or external memory backups—miniature neural clouds to archive less-relevant memories while keeping your core self intact. ("Download my 2200s life memories to external storage—I need brain space for my alien linguistics course.")

Then there's decision fatigue. We already get tired choosing what to eat. What happens when you've made decisions for three centuries straight? Choosing a favorite ice cream flavor could become a decade-long existential crisis. "In 2082, I loved mint-choco-chip. But then came the Great Mango Craze of 2174..."

In short: a 300-year brain wouldn't just be a smarter brain. It'd be a different brain. More layered, more organized, possibly more peaceful—or more eccentric.

But one thing's for sure: you'd never run out of things to think about.

Earth with Old Tiny Creatures (That's You)

Now let's zoom out and look at the big picture. If everyone lives to 300, the planet's population would balloon unless people have fewer kids. Which means family trees would start to look like forests. Your great-great-great-grandfather might still be alive and possibly still winning chess tournaments.

Careers would also change. You could have five careers in one lifetime. Start as an astronaut, shift to art, run a deep-sea kelp farm, become a historian, and finally retire as a professional cloud sculptor on Mars.

But wait—retire? When? At 200? 250? Would governments push retirement age to 280? "Congratulations on completing your 250th year of service. You're now eligible for one year of pension!"

And education? A 300-year lifespan means forever learning. You could spend 50 years just exploring ancient Greek philosophy before you even touch quantum computing.

Society: Slower, Smarter, or Just More Tired?

With long life comes long responsibility. (Maybe)

Democracy might evolve into something more... patient. Imagine debates where people remember laws from 180 years ago. Wars might become rarer—after all, who wants to fight when you still have 180 years of vacation planned?

But social progress might slow. People who lived through ten different generations might resist change. "Back in 2235, we didn't have teleporters! Kids these days don't appreciate anything!"

However, wiser, more experienced humans might also make better leaders. (Unless they're clinging to power for 150 years. Yikes.)

Could Science Actually Make This Happen?

Short answer: maybe. Sort of. Someday.

Scientists today are already poking at the boundaries of aging. Some cool stuff that might one day extend human life dramatically:

CRISPR: Gene-editing tools that might fix aging-related mutations.

Senolytics: Drugs that destroy old, zombie-like cells that clog up our bodies.

Epigenetic reprogramming: Turning back the clock on cells, literally.

Brain-machine interfaces: What if you could upload your brain into the cloud and never age?

But living to 300 isn't just a matter of science. It's also about ethics, sustainability, and whether we should do it even if we can.

Plot Twist: Would You Want To?

Okay, let's be honest. Living to 300 might sound amazing at first. But think about it—300 birthdays. 300 times people sing "Happy Birthday" slightly off-key. 300 years of taxes. Would life feel precious if you had forever? Would love still feel urgent? Would achievements still matter if you had three centuries to get around to them?

Maybe, just maybe, it's our ticking clock that makes life feel magical.

Final Thought: Legacy Over Longevity?

So what if we don't evolve to live for 300 years? Maybe we don't need to. Maybe the better question is: How can we make the years we do have count? Whether you live for 80 years or 300, it's not the length of life that matters most.

It's the story you write while you're here.

And hey, if you're still reading this at age 273—thanks for sticking around.

XVII

What If We Had To Generate Our Own Electricity To Survive?

Okay, deep breath: the power grid is gone. No coal, no solar farms, no sneaky wall sockets pumping silent volts into your life. Your phone? Dead. Your fridge? Warm. Your gaming console? Tragically, heartbreakingly black-screened. And here's the kicker: from now on, you only get electricity if you generate it.

Let's be clear—this isn't some fitness-tracking app trying to guilt you into walking more. This is survival. If you want light to read at night, you pedal. If you want toast? Get cranking. Want to charge your laptop? Hope your thighs are ready for a Tour de France-level workout. Electricity is no longer a background thing you ignore until the bill shows up. It's your own full-time job now.

The Human Battery: How Much Power Can We Make?

So, how much electricity can you generate?

Let's say you hop on a stationary bike hooked up to a generator. If you're reasonably fit (and not faking leg cramps), you might produce 100 watts per hour. That's enough to:

Power a lightbulb

Charge a phone

Toast one slice of bread? – Not a chance (seriously—your toaster eats 800 watts/hour. That's like 8 hours of cycling for one slice of sourdough.)

Want to take a hot shower? That's about 4,000 watts for just 10 minutes. Which means: time to get used to cold showers, or pedal like you're being chased by a lightning bolt.

The average person uses around 30,000 watts a day through appliances, lighting, heating, and the occasional binge-watch session. So, if you're generating power all by yourself, your lifestyle's about to shrink faster than a dying phone battery.

Power Budgeting Becomes A Thing

Budget? That quite doesn't match with us, does it?

In this new world, every electrical decision becomes a life decision. Do you want light to study tonight or heat to not freeze? Phone charge or microwave dinner? Your smartwatch better come with budgeting software—not for money, but for watts.

Families might divide duties:

Mom pedals for the oven.

Dad runs on a treadmill to charge the Wi-Fi router.

The kids? Tiny wheels for their tablets.

Sleepovers would be less about popcorn and movies and more like underground power co-ops:

"You bring the popcorn. I'll bring the leg muscles."

And forget binge-watching. You'll be binge-walking just to earn an hour (or maybe less)of Netflix.

Wearable Tech Gets... Sweaty

You've seen smartwatches. Now meet smart-socks with built-in piezoelectric generators. Every step you take sends tiny jolts of electricity into your personal battery bank. Joggers and dancers suddenly become society's elite. Gym class turns into a national service.

Even clothes evolve. Your hoodie might have nano-fibers that absorb motion and heat. Every awkward shrug or dramatic eye-roll? Pure electricity, baby.

And don't forget hand-crank chargers. Your backpack might come with retractable crank arms, so while your friends talk during lunch, you're just there like:

"Can't talk. Gotta generate enough power to unlock my fridge."

Homes, Reimagined

Your house becomes a cross between a power plant and a medieval cottage.

You'd have:

Floor tiles that generate electricity when you wal

Exercise machines in every room (finally, a reason to use that dusty elliptical)

Manual-powered blenders, fans, even TVs with crank handles

Sleep wouldn't just recharge you—it'd be a strategic loss. "I could sleep… or pedal for another 40 minutes and get two hours of laptop time."

Entire cities might redesign around power efficiency. Elevators replaced with ramps and pulley systems. Movie theaters powered by the audience pedaling as they watch. (Spoiler: action scenes = more pedaling.)

No Power = No Perks (Or Survival)

This isn't just about charging your gadgets. If your heart needs a pacemaker or your lungs need a ventilator, you need power to survive. That means medical technology becomes dependent on constant human-generated electricity. Hospitals might have entire floors of volunteers cycling in shifts, powering life-saving machines. People might donate "watts" instead of blood. You might even carry a power ID:

"Hi, I'm Alex. Blood type: O+. Muscle type: High endurance. Can sprint-charge a defibrillator in under 3 minutes."

Power becomes currency. A "kilowatt economy" emerges. You get paid in watts, and bills come in volts. "Sorry, I can't afford a microwave meal tonight. I'm 10 watts short for my target this week!"

Would We All Become Eco-Heroes?

Funny thing is, a world like this might be the greenest Earth has ever seen.

No coal, no gas, no giant data centers slurping up power like smoothie machines. Just millions of sweaty, grunting humans keeping the lights on—one awkward push-up at a time.

People would think twice before wasting energy. No more leaving lights on. No more charging ten devices you don't use. Want to play video games all night? Sure. Hope your quads are ready.

Carbon footprints? More like calorie footprints.

Climate change? Reversing itself while we collectively burn our body fat to cook dinner.

And gyms? Oh, gyms would become temples. Literal powerhouses. New social norm:

"Hey, wanna hang out at the gym later?"

"Sure, I'm trying to earn enough electricity for a bubble bath."

The Bright Side

Sure, it sounds exhausting. But maybe we'd be healthier, more grateful, and weirdly proud. Power would no longer be invisible. It would have weight. Cost. Sweat. Effort

And when you finally flip on a tiny desk lamp at night, knowing you powered it yourself—that tiny, warm glow would feel like victory.

Unless, of course, your brother unplugs it by accident. Then he better start running. You've got electricity to make—and revenge to plan.

The Final Thought

If we really had to generate our own electricity to survive, it wouldn't just be a shift in how we power our gadgets—it would be a total revolution in how we live, work, and think.

Imagine a world where energy is no longer something abstract that flows invisibly through wires but something personal. Something you feel in your legs after an hour on the bike, or in your back after carrying a generator-laced backpack up five flights of stairs. In this reality, electricity becomes as intimate as food and water—something you earn, something you respect, and something you can't waste without real consequences.

We'd probably become fitter, yes, but we'd also become more conscious. Every action would have an energy cost, and suddenly, convenience would come with a price tag written in sweat. Want to scroll through memes for an hour? Hope you powered up your phone with a morning jog. Want warm soup on a winter evening? Better gather the family for a power-generating dance party in the living room. This isn't just about muscles—it's about mindset.

And perhaps, just perhaps, we'd become more empathetic too. We'd understand what it means to work for light, for heat, for comfort. We'd stop taking things like refrigeration or clean water pumps for granted. People in remote villages today already know what that struggle feels like. In this world, we'd all walk a mile (or pedal it) in their shoes.

Technologically, humans might innovate faster than ever. Instead of building bigger power plants, we'd aim for smarter, more efficient tools. Devices that run on less, survive longer, and do more with almost nothing. Sustainability wouldn't be a buzzword—it would be a necessity. Wastefulness would be socially unacceptable. The person who left the fan running while not in the room? That's the new public enemy. "Energy leeching" might become an actual crime.

Socially, we might start valuing people in new ways. The strongest legs in your household might become more valuable than a degree. Schools could grade students not just on academic performance but on their power output. You could literally earn your education—pedal for two hours, unlock two classes. Think of it as physical scholarship.

On a broader level, we'd start redesigning our entire world. Cities would sprawl around kinetic energy zones. Entire transportation systems might be human-powered hybrids—trains that need people to jog in central gyms to keep the engine moving. It sounds absurd now, but remember, the idea of a flying machine once seemed laughable too.

But perhaps the biggest change wouldn't be technological or physical—it would be emotional.

We'd come to see energy as something sacred, something earned with real effort. A simple night lamp glowing beside your bed wouldn't be just a convenience—it would be a triumph. A reward. A proof that you moved, lived, breathed, and powered your own existence.

And in that world, maybe we'd all be a little less lazy... and a lot more alive.

So next time you plug in your phone or switch on a light, pause for just a second.

Ask yourself:

"What if I had to power this?"

And maybe—just maybe—you'll feel a tiny jolt of gratitude.

The best kind of energy there is.

XVIII

What If Humans Never Needed To Sleep?

Okay, let's get this out of the way: I love sleep.

I mean, who doesn't? That glorious moment when you don't have to think, don't have to do math homework, and your only job is to turn into a human burrito and drift off into unconsciousness while your brain plays some bizarre indie film called "dreams."

But here's the twist—what if we never needed to sleep? Not like, we couldn't, but more like our bodies and brains simply didn't need it at all. Ever. Like, biologically, we were designed to go 24/7, no recharge required.

Let's just say that if that were true, I wouldn't be writing this at 11:47 p.m. with eye bags heavier than my school bag. So, in this very serious, slightly sleep-deprived exploration, we're going to look at what life—and biology—might look like in a world where humans never, ever needed to sleep.

First Things First: Why Do We Even Sleep?

Before we delete sleep from existence, let's appreciate the science of why it exists in the first place. Sleep is not just something our lazy teenage selves invented to avoid chores

Sleep is essential for:

Brain Function: During sleep, the brain literally cleans itself. It flushes out waste proteins through something called the glymphatic system. Think of it as a nightly rinse cycle for your brain.

Memory Consolidation: Sleep helps us turn short-term memories into long-term ones. So technically, that all-nighter before the exam? Useless. Your brain wasn't saving any of that info.

Growth and Repair: Growth hormone is released during deep sleep, which is why kids are always told to sleep more. Apparently, height doesn't come from Netflix.

Immune Boosting: A good night's sleep strengthens your immune system. Less sleep = more colds = more gross tissue piles on your desk.

Mood Regulation: You know how you want to fight the toaster when you're sleep-deprived? That's not just crankiness; your brain literally loses emotional control.

So yeah, sleep is kind of a big deal.

Now Imagine: Sleep Doesn't Exist Anymore

Alright, now for the real fun. Let's pull a Thanos on sleep and snap it out of existence. What happens then?

Well, for starters, humans would be biologically engineered to function perfectly 24/7. That means:

No melatonin making us drowsy.

No circadian rhythms keeping us tied to the sun.

No drooping eyelids in physics class (wait, that might be a downside—how else do we pretend we're concentrating?).

But more importantly, we'd need some serious biological upgrades. Let me break down what those might look like.

1. The Brain: Fully Awake, Forever?

Currently, our brains need about 7–9 hours to rest and reset. Without sleep, the brain would have to:

Clean itself while awake (real-time glymphatic system?)

Process emotions live, without the REM sleep "therapy" session

Store memories instantly, like auto-saving a document every second

Manage attention, focus, and learning with zero breaks

We'd need a brain that's basically a NASA-level supercomputer. No overheating. No lag. No "Oops, I forgot what I was saying mid-sent—"

Also, that thing where your brain replays stuff during dreams to process emotions? That'd have to happen in real-time too. Which means you might just be crying over your math test while doing your math test. Efficient, but awkward.

2. Energy Levels: Where's the Battery?

Our bodies use sleep to restore energy—ATP (adenosine triphosphate) builds back up while we snooze. So without sleep, the body would need a constant energy supply.

That means:

Our metabolism would have to be super-efficient.

Maybe we'd need built-in power-saving modes, like your laptop.

Or better yet, we'd probably evolve to use solar energy, like plants. I don't know about you, but becoming a semi-photosynthetic human sounds kind of cool. Imagine charging up while chilling at the park.

On the flip side, we'd need to eat a lot more. Because calories = energy. And no rest means more energy spent. So instead of three meals a day, we might need six or seven. Midnight snacks would become mandatory.

3. The Body Clock: RIP Circadian Rhythm

Right now, our bodies follow a 24-hour cycle, synced with sunlight. Hormones, temperature, digestion—they all follow this rhythm. Without sleep, that rhythm would be irrelevant.

So...

Offices, schools, and shops might be open 24/7.

You could go to the dentist at 2 a.m. (creepy, but convenient).

Night and day would lose their meaning. Time itself would become... flexible.

Think about it. A society with no standard bedtime. People doing homework at 3 a.m., jogging at midnight, grocery shopping at dawn.

Basically, society would look like one giant airport.

The Social Side: What Would Life Be Like?

Now let's go full sci-fi and imagine the social side of this no-sleep world.

1. More Time = More Productivity?

On paper, having 8 extra hours a day sounds amazing. That's 56 extra hours a week. You could:

Learn 3 languages

Watch every Marvel movie twice

Actually do your homework

But here's the catch: capitalism never sleeps. If we don't need to rest, companies might expect us to work longer. Instead of 9–5 jobs, we might get stuck in 16-hour work shifts. Yay, progress?

Also, school could go on for 12 hours. I can feel your soul dying already.

2. Mental Health: Better or Worse?

Some might argue that without sleep, we'd be emotionally stable all the time. No sleep deprivation = no mood swings, right? But let's be honest. Constant wakefulness could be overstimulating. Imagine your brain having zero quiet time. Always thinking, always working, always interacting.

No break. No pause.

We might need to invent digital meditation pods where people can simulate peace and quiet. Or we'd all just start staring at walls for an hour a day, pretending we're asleep. Like a fake nap. A "flap"?

3. Relationships Would Change

No sleep means more time with people. That could be great—or a nightmare.

Roommates: "We've been talking for 23 straight hours. Please stop."

Parents: "Why didn't you study during the night? You had all the time in the world."

Siblings: "You were supposed to stop talking at midnight. It's 5 a.m. Go fake-nap or something."

Basically, we'd have to invent personal boundaries again. Probably in the form of a universal rule: "Thou shalt not talk to anyone between 2 a.m. and 4 a.m. unless it's about aliens."

The Upsides (Yes, There Are Some)

Let's be fair. There would be a few amazing upsides.

1. No More Snoring

That's it. That's the win.

2. No More Alarms

No more heart attacks at 6:30 a.m. No more "five more minutes" that turn into "oops, I missed the bus."

3. Safety and Security

Imagine emergency services that never need rest. Doctors, pilots, firefighters—always alert, always ready. No fatigue-related accidents.

Also, parents could take care of babies in shifts without getting sleep-deprived. That's a parenting revolution right there.

But Wait... Would We Even Be Human?

Here's the philosophical twist (yes, I'm going there):

Would we still be us if we never slept?

Dreams, rest, unconsciousness—these are not just breaks. They're part of how we understand life. Dreams inspire art, inventions, and bizarre conspiracy theories.

Sleep gives us time away from the world—a safe little reboot. Even boredom, even stillness, has value.

Without sleep, life would be faster, longer, louder—but would it be better? Would we still enjoy books and movies if we never took a break from reality? Would we appreciate silence if the world never slept?

Would we even remember how to dream?

Final Thoughts from a Sleepy Student

So, what if humans never needed to sleep?

We'd gain time. We'd revolutionize biology. We'd redesign society from the ground up. But in doing so, we might lose the magic of night—the dreams, the peace, the stillness. We'd have to invent new ways to rest, recharge, and find calm.

So, while it's fun to imagine a world without sleep, maybe it's not so bad that we need to shut down every night. After all, some of the best parts of life happen between dreams and dawn.

Let's get some sleep, shall we?

Goodnight.

(Or not.)

XIX

What If The Universe Had An Edge?

So, picture this: you're in a rocket ship—because obviously, who isn't in a rocket ship in their free time—and you're flying through space. Past the planets, past the Kuiper Belt, past Voyager 1 waving at you like, "You're not supposed to be here."

You keep going. Past the Milky Way. Past galaxies that look like glitter spilled on black velvet. And finally, after traveling for billions of light years...

You hit The Edge.

Like—bonk—the universe just... ends.

Wait. What?

That's the question I've been obsessing over: What if the universe actually had an edge? A real boundary. A cosmic "Sorry, we're closed" sign.

Let's unpack this cosmic headache with a little help from physics, philosophy, and the occasional space joke.

First, What Is the Universe?

Before we go looking for the edge of the universe, let's be clear about what we're dealing with.

The observable universe is about 93 billion light-years across. That's the part we can see, based on how far light has traveled since the Big Bang (~13.8 billion years ago). But that doesn't mean that's all there is. In fact, most scientists believe the universe is either infinite or so big it might as well be. Like the size of my syllabus, but with fewer chapter tests.

Now here's the tricky bit: the universe isn't like a planet or a box—it doesn't exist in space, it is space. So asking "Where does it end?" is like asking "Where does the surface of a balloon end?"

(Spoiler: it doesn't—it wraps around.)

But let's say, for fun, that it does end. What would that mean?

Would you just... walk into a giant "Now Leaving the Universe" sign?

Would there be a velvet rope and a bored cosmic security guard saying, "Sorry, kids, no peeking beyond this point"?

Or would you bump into an invisible wall, like some intergalactic video game boundary, and awkwardly slide along it like your character's stuck?

And what's beyond that edge?

Is there a giant blank canvas?

A multiverse airport terminal where other universes are boarding?

A cosmic break room where space-time takes a nap?

Here's another brain bender: if the universe has an edge, then doesn't that mean there must be something outside the universe?

But "outside" the universe doesn't really make sense—because space and time themselves are inside the universe. Outside of space and time, there's no "place" for anything to be. It's like asking what's north of the North Pole. (Answer: nothing, just cold and penguins... okay, no penguins—they live in the South.)

And if the universe were a bubble, what's the bubble in? Bubble wrap?

Now, most scientists lean toward the idea that the universe is boundless—not because it goes on forever in every direction like an eternal Walmart aisle, but because it curves in on itself in a way that doesn't require an "outside." Kinda like a 3D version of the surface of Earth: you can keep going forever without falling off the edge.

So the more we ask "Where's the end?", the more the universe seems to whisper back, "You're asking the wrong question."

Because maybe the universe doesn't end.

Maybe it just... keeps unfolding, like a cosmic scroll, expanding not into space—but creating space itself as it grows.

And maybe, just maybe, the real edge isn't out there at all—

It's in here: the edge of what we can observe, measure, imagine.

The rest?

It's waiting. For our questions.

For our curiosity.

For our next big telescope to squint into the great unknown and say:

"Hey, what's that over there?"

Scenario #1: The Brick Wall Model

Let's go old-school. Imagine you're flying through space and suddenly—BAM! You hit a wall. A real, solid cosmic brick wall.

That's the "hard edge" theory.

What's beyond it? No one knows. Maybe:

A void of absolute nothingness (not even space or time)

A loading screen that says "Next Universe Coming Soon"

Or my personal favorite: a giant sign saying "You've reached the end of the universe. Please turn back."

But here's the problem:

If there's a wall, then... what's holding it up? What is it made of? Who built it? And if you touch it—what happens?

According to physics as we know it, this is... unlikely. The universe doesn't seem to have physical boundaries. It's more like a curved surface expanding in all directions. So if you go far enough, you don't hit a wall—you just keep going.

Scenario #2: The Loop Theory

Okay, let's try something trippier. What if the universe has an edge because it loops back on itself?

Imagine walking in a straight line on Earth. Eventually, you'll end up where you started (unless you fall into the ocean or get distracted by a street vendor selling momos). Now apply that to space. Maybe the universe is finite but unbounded—like a 3D version of a sphere. So if you fly straight long enough, you end up back at your starting point.

That's what Einstein suggested with his idea of a closed universe. It doesn't have an edge; it's just shaped in a way that feels endless.

So technically, in this model, the edge of the universe is... you again. Congratulations, you're the center of everything. (Don't let it go to your head.)

Scenario #3: The Multiverse Border

Now let's go full science fiction.

What if the edge of the universe isn't a wall or a loop—but a door?

Some scientists theorize that we might live in a multiverse—an ocean of bubble universes, each with its own laws of physics. In that case, the edge of our universe could be like the surface of a bubble, and right next door is another universe with its own weird rules.

Maybe gravity pulls things sideways

Maybe time runs backwards

Maybe pineapples do belong on pizza (terrifying)

Could we ever reach that border? The answer is: probably not. The distance, radiation, and lack of snacks make inter-universal travel slightly impractical.

But hey, maybe advanced civilizations figured it out. Maybe UFOs are just tourists from Universe B, stopping by to see how weird ours is.

But Hold Up: What Would an Edge Feel Like?

Let's say, somehow, you reach the actual edge of the universe. What would you see?

Would it look like:

A glowing curtain of quantum energy?

A glitchy cosmic firewall like in a video game?

The end credits of reality, starring "Dark Matter" as itself?

Honestly, no one knows. Because here's the wild thing: edges require space to exist beyond them. But space itself might just... stop. Like, literally. No space. No time. No dimensions. Just a boundary between everything and nothing.

Kind of makes you want to sit in a corner and question reality, right?

Scientific Implications: Would the Edge Matter?

Here's where the real science comes in. If the universe did have an edge, it would rewrite our entire understanding of cosmology.

1. General Relativity Would Get Complicated

Einstein's equations rely on space being smooth and continuous. An edge would break that smoothness—kind of like a hole in your socks.

2. Conservation Laws Might Break

What happens to energy, mass, and momentum at the edge? Do they reflect off it? Vanish? Get stored for later use?

3. Cosmic Expansion Would Be Weird

Currently, space itself is expanding. But what if it can't expand past the edge? Would the expansion stop? Bounce back? Create a cosmic pressure cooker?

These questions are so strange that most scientists avoid them by assuming: "There is no edge. Period."

So... Could We Ever Find the Edge?

Even if it exists, finding the edge is like trying to find the last page in a book that keeps adding pages as you read it.

Why?

Because the universe is expanding faster than the speed of light. That means there are parts we will never reach or see. Ever. Light from those regions will literally never catch up. In fact, the farther you look, the faster things are moving away. It's like chasing someone in a car, but their car gets faster every time you blink.

So even if there is an edge, it's beyond the cosmic speed limit. No GPS, telescope, or intergalactic Uber is going to get us there.

But Let's Pretend We Did

Okay, back to imagination mode.

Let's say we did reach the edge. We take a selfie. We post it: "At the edge of the universe—#NoFilter #LiterallyNothingHere."

What happens next?

Would we:

Discover other dimensions?

Fall into an alternate timeline?

Start the next Big Bang by poking the wrong quantum string?

Or maybe, just maybe—we'd realize that the edge isn't something out there.

Maybe the edge is a limit of human understanding. A border our brains can't cross yet. Until we evolve further.

Or until we invent quantum nachos that open portals. Whichever comes first.

Philosophical Time: Does the Edge Even Matter?

Some philosophers (and tired students) argue that the question of an edge is like asking, "What's north of the North Pole?"

The answer: nothing. Because north ends there. The pole defines the top.

Maybe the universe is the same. There's no "outside," because the universe is all there is. It defines existence.

So asking, "What's beyond the edge?" might be like a goldfish asking, "What's beyond the bowl?" The fish doesn't have the brainpower to imagine Netflix, gravity, and pizza rolls.

Maybe we're the goldfish.

Final Thoughts

So, what if the universe had an edge?

Well...

Physics would panic. Scientists would throw their coffee.

Instagram would be full of "I Found the Edge of Space" dance videos.

But most importantly: we still wouldn't know what's beyond it.

And maybe that's the best part. Maybe the mystery is what makes space so cool. Maybe we're meant to keep exploring—not just outwards, but inwards, into the limits of what we can imagine.

So until we find that edge—or prove it doesn't exist—I'll keep staring at the night sky wondering:

What's out there?

And why hasn't anyone sent us a cosmic "Welcome to the Edge" postcard yet?

XX

What If The World Was Controlled By Kids?

A one-word answer from the adults - Havoc. But is it really all about havoc?

Let's dive in.

1. The Great Kid Takeover

It began on a Tuesday. Why Tuesday? Nobody knows. But one thing is certain: on that oddly quiet morning, every adult on Earth suddenly—and mysteriously—fell into a deep sleep. Teachers slumped onto their desks mid-lecture, parents dozed off over breakfast, presidents face-planted into their microphones, and scientists... well, they were snoring next to half-finished experiments.

Kids all over the world blinked, looked around, and realized: "Wait. We're in charge now?"

Within hours, world history had taken a hard left turn. Schools were declared "optional fun zones," broccoli was banned internationally, and the first Presidential TikTok Challenge was announced. The Age of Adults had ended. The Kid Era had begun.

But what would this new world look like if kids actually ran it—not just for a day, but for years? Would it be all candy and cartoons—or something surprisingly smart? Let's dive into this strange, science-flavored scenario.

2. The Day the Grown-Ups Disappeared

Scientists (before they fell asleep) might've blamed a sudden energy wave from a rogue neutron star or an alien experiment gone wrong. Whatever the cause, adults across the globe slipped into a harmless coma-like sleep. Unharmed but unresponsive. Poof—gone from daily life.

Panic? A little. But mostly... party. At first, kids raided candy stores, skateboarded through malls, and hosted worldwide Zoom dance-offs. But soon, questions popped up:

Who would run the power plants?
Who would fix the Internet?
Who would decide the rules?

A global emergency meeting was held—on Discord, naturally—and the decision was made: a World Kid Government would form, featuring representatives aged 6 to 17. The motto? "Fair, Fun, and Full of Fizz."

3. Welcome to Kidtopia

In the new world, schools were redesigned into hybrid play-labs. Slide tunnels replaced hallways, math was taught through video games, and lunch was served by robot vending machines designed by 13-year-old coders. Homework was abolished. Instead, kids did "mission quests" like designing a hoverboard or building a soap-powered rocket.

But without adult supervision, something else changed—health.

Scientific studies (from the brave few teens still doing science) showed that endless sugar caused hyperactivity, which led to poor sleep cycles. Without structured sleep, kids' circadian rhythms went wild. Some woke up at 2 AM, others refused to sleep at all. Melatonin gummies became the new bedtime currency.

Nutritionists (now 12-year-olds with lab coats and Google access) discovered that a 100% junk food diet caused weird side effects: glowing teeth, neon-colored poop, and spontaneous dance battles due to sugar spikes.

Clearly, a balance had to be found. So a new rule was passed: "For every bag of chips, one banana smoothie must be consumed." Compromise.

4. *The New Governments*

The United Nations (now renamed the "United Playstations") held its first session in Minecraft. Delegates from every country logged into a giant blocky courtroom, wearing custom skins—some were dragons, others were wizards. Resolutions were passed by parkour votes: if you could complete the obstacle course, your law stood.

New laws included:

Mandatory nap time after lunch (except on Fridays).

Equal access to popsicles in all climates.

A ban on boring speeches longer than 5 minutes.

Cognitive science tells us that kids' prefrontal cortex—the part of the brain that handles planning and long-term thinking—is still developing. This led to very creative, but often impulsive decisions. One country banned homework; another declared every Thursday "Dress Like a Superhero Day."

Interestingly, some nations thrived. Empathy and fairness ruled. Fights were settled by Mario Kart races. Kids showed a remarkable ability to care about fairness and fun at the same time.

5. Toys, Tech, and Transportation

The adult-designed roads were too boring. So 9-year-old engineers revamped transportation: buses became roller coasters with seatbelts, skateboards had AI voice assistants, and cars had bounce features like trampolines.

One team in Japan developed a drone that delivered cupcakes using GPS and voice command: "Hey YumBot, bring me red velvet!"

Safety? Well... not perfect. Without adult engineers to double-check designs, there were a few "bouncy bus" accidents. But kids quickly learned the value of physics and materials science—because if your cardboard bridge collapses, you really want to know about tensile strength.

Amusement parks doubled as research labs. "The more fun, the more learning," said 11-year-old scientist Tara Patel, who built a solar-powered seesaw that created electricity every time it moved.

6. Ice Cream Economy and Glitter Fuel

With adults gone, money felt... boring. So kids reinvented the economy. The most popular currency? Ice cream scoops.

1 scoop = 1 basic toy

5 scoops = 1 hour of video game time

100 scoops = a hoverboard

To manage inflation, they created "melting taxes." If you didn't use your ice cream money fast, it melted—literally. Economists (now ages 13 to 16) learned fast about scarcity, value, and time decay.

As for science and energy, traditional fuel sources were abandoned. New "kid-powered" ideas included:

Candy-fueled cars: worked, but attracted ants.

Glitter-reactor: exploded once, covered half of London in sparkle dust.

Banana peel biofuel: surprisingly efficient and eco-friendly!

Kids learned the basics of chemistry, thermodynamics, and biology—all in the name of fun. Many ended up being better scientists than the adults they replaced.

7. A Planet Run by Play

With kids in charge, something amazing happened. Climate change action skyrocketed. Plastic straws were banned. Forests became protected game zones. A new initiative, "Plant-a-Tree-Get-a-Snack," led to over 1 billion new trees planted in just six months.

Why? Because kids like animals. They care about the oceans. And they wanted to save the polar bears before they disappeared (because those plushies were based on real animals, after all!).

There were still problems. Some kids didn't agree on the rules. Internet trolls became literal monsters in virtual spaces. And without adults to mediate, a few online games led to real-world arguments.

But overall, the world became kinder, more playful, and way more colorful. Giant chalk drawings decorated highways. Robots danced on command. Playgrounds stretched across cities like vines.

8. The Return of the Adults

One day, exactly one year after it all began, adults started waking up.

They were groggy. Confused. And slightly embarrassed to learn that while they were out cold, their kids ran the entire world—and didn't completely mess it up.

Sure, a few libraries had been turned into Nerf arenas. Yes, someone accidentally launched a soda-powered rocket into the Moon Museum. But overall? The planet was cleaner, people were happier, and science was cooler than ever.

Instead of taking back control, adults decided to listen. They joined hands with the new Kid Council and formed a hybrid government. Rules were now tested by adults—but also fun-checked by kids.

One parent said, "We've been so focused on keeping kids safe, we forgot how much they have to teach us."

9. So... Should Kids Rule the World?

Now, let's get real. Scientifically, kids have amazing creativity, curiosity, and compassion. But their brains are still developing, especially in areas that handle risk and long-term consequences. That's why a mix of childlike wonder and adult experience may be the best combo.

Still, imagine a world where:

Kids help design playground cities.

Laws are explained with comics.

Schools encourage questions, not just answers.

We may not want 6-year-olds in charge of nuclear codes... but maybe we do want them helping to redesign society's rules—with more kindness, more play, and more possibility.

Final Thought

Think about it—kids have brains wired for curiosity, imagination, and rapid learning. Their minds are like sponges, absorbing new ideas and making wild connections that adults often miss. Scientists call this neuroplasticity—the brain's ability to change and grow—which is at its peak in childhood and adolescence. This is why kids can invent new games, learn languages quickly, and find creative solutions to problems that sometimes stump adults.

But kids also see the world differently. Where adults might see rules and limits, kids see possibilities and "What ifs." Their thinking isn't weighed down by years of routine or worry about "how things have always been done." Instead, they ask questions like, "Why can't cars fly?" or "What if schools were made of candy?" These questions may sound silly, but they're exactly the kind of thinking that leads to breakthroughs.

Of course, kids' brains are still developing, especially in areas responsible for planning, controlling impulses, and considering consequences. That's why some kid-led decisions might seem chaotic or risky. But isn't that part of innovation? Trying, failing, learning, and trying again?

Without risk, there's no progress.

The kid-controlled world we imagined shows us a balance: the energy, enthusiasm, and creativity of youth combined with the wisdom and experience of adults. What if we didn't wait for the kids to take over the world to listen to them? What if schools, governments, and companies involved young people in real decisions, harnessing their fresh ideas while guiding them with knowledge?

Science shows that involving kids in problem-solving helps develop their critical thinking and empathy. It creates future leaders who are not only smart but also compassionate and creative. And the world desperately needs leaders like that—people who can imagine a better future and work together to build it.

So maybe the real lesson here isn't about kids ruling the world alone. It's about sharing power, respect, and responsibility across generations. About remembering that the future belongs to everyone—from the youngest thinkers to the oldest dreamers.

And who knows? Maybe the next great invention, policy, or solution could come from a 7-year-old with a wild idea and a big heart.

Because in the end, the best way to shape the future...

...might just be to let the future help shape it.

So, what would you do if you were in charge?

And Here Comes The Bonus Chapter

XXI

What If Every Action You Take Creates A New Universe?

It all started with pizza.

You were standing in front of the counter, hungry, staring at two choices: Margherita or Pepperoni. The pressure was real. You picked Pepperoni, took a bite, and life went on.

Or did it?

According to one mind-melting scientific theory, the moment you chose pepperoni over Margherita, the universe split in two.

In one universe, you're munching pepperoni.

In another? You're enjoying gooey, cheesy Margherita.

In yet another, you walked out and got a burrito instead.

And in another, the pizza shop turned out to be a spaceship run by time-traveling cats.

Wait. What?!

Welcome to the Many-Worlds Interpretation—a real, serious theory in physics that suggests every possible outcome of every decision actually happens, but in a different universe.

Let's break this multiverse open.

The Science: Many Worlds, One You (Kind Of)

The idea comes from quantum mechanics—the science of how tiny particles like electrons and atoms behave. And spoiler alert: they behave weirdly. Quantum particles can exist in more than one state at once. This is called superposition. Imagine flipping a coin and it being both heads and tails until you actually look at it. That's how quantum particles live their lives—always undecided until someone observes them.

Now here's where it gets crazier.

When someone observes the particle, it seems to "choose" one outcome. But physicist Hugh Everett in 1957 had a different idea. He said: "What if... the universe doesn't choose? What if... both outcomes happen—but in separate universes?"

Boom. This became the Many-Worlds Interpretation.

So every time a quantum decision is made—like whether a particle spins this way or that—the universe splits, creating a copy for each possibility.

Now think bigger.

You are made of quantum particles. So is your brain. So are your decisions. That means every time you decide to go left or right, eat cereal or pancakes, text your friend or not...You're splitting the universe.

The Multiverse Is... Crowded

Let's say you make 100 decisions a day. (That's a low guess.) That's 100 splits.

Now multiply that by 8 billion people on Earth. Now add every ant, bacteria, and robot vacuum making choices too. And don't forget particles doing quantum flips billions of times per second.

Yeah.

That's a lot of universes. Like, infinite universes. A multiverse so big it makes your head feel like it's doing quantum flips.

But don't worry—you don't feel the split. You just keep living your life, unaware that another version of you just did something totally different. Like wore the blue shirt. Or became a pro ice skater. Or accidentally started a pancake cult.

And that version of you thinks they're the real one.

Wild, right?

Would You Meet Your Other Yous?

Let's say you had a Multiverse Portal™ that let you peek into those other realities.

In one universe, you're a billionaire who invented eco-friendly hoverboots.In another, you never moved cities and became a local hero for rescuing baby pandas.In another, you're a world-famous beatboxer with a pet flamingo.

And guess what? They're all you.

Same DNA. Same early memories. But after each decision, your paths split further and further. One little choice—like joining dance class or skipping it—could lead to a completely different life.

Makes you think twice before skipping that opportunity, huh?

Butterflies and Chaos

This ties into something called the Butterfly Effect, part of chaos theory. It says a tiny action—like a butterfly flapping its wings in Brazil—might cause a tornado in Texas weeks later. In the multiverse, this means tiny decisions ripple across realities. Say "hi" to someone? Maybe that leads to a friendship that leads to starting a company that cures disease. Don't say "hi"? That reality never happens. A whole new universe blooms—or fades—based on your smallest move.

The power you hold is incredible.

What About the Regret Universes?

Ever had a thought like, "What if I had done things differently?"

In the multiverse theory, you did—just in another universe.

Maybe in Universe-900K, you studied piano instead of coding, and you're performing in Paris. Or maybe in Universe-42X, you said "yes" to pineapple on pizza and regretted everything.

These "regret universes" aren't just fantasy—they could be real, running parallel to this one, starring other yous.

But here's a comforting thought: those "other yous" probably wonder what it would've been like to be you.

Because to them, your life is the road not taken.

Can You Talk to Your Other Selves?

Now this gets juicy.

Let's say we invent a quantum communicator. Could we call our alternate selves?

In theory, no. Each universe is completely separate. They don't "interact."But... some scientists wonder if certain quantum particles can "entangle" across universes, creating tiny overlaps.

If that's true—and it's a BIG if—we might someday be able to:

Send messages to other versions of ourselves

Transfer knowledge across realities

Or even merge realities (gulp)

Just imagine: one day, you might remember a skill you never learned... because another you did.

Whoa.

What Happens If You Stop Making Decisions?

Let's say you decide to sit still and make zero choices.

Would the universe stop splitting?

Short answer: Nope.

Because your body is still making decisions at the molecular and quantum level. Your cells divide, your neurons fire, your atoms dance. Even blinking or breathing—those are micro-decisions.

So unless you stop existing, the universe keeps multiplying around you.

In other words: you can't stop the multiverse train.

Does This Make You the Center of the Multiverse?

Not exactly. Every particle, every person, every blade of grass is also creating new universes. But here's the amazing part: You are the only "you" in this particular universe. That means your choices here still matter. A lot. Just because there are infinite versions of you doesn't mean this one doesn't count.

Think of it this way:

If every version of you is a note in a grand symphony of existence, You are still the only one playing your unique tune in this reality.

So play it well.

Are There Dark Universes?

Probably.

If some universes go better than yours, some will go... worse.

There could be worlds where things didn't work out. Where your big risks failed. Where you lost friends, made mistakes, or became the villain in someone else's story. It's a sobering thought—but also a reminder: In this universe, you still have the chance to choose. To change. To try.

You don't need a reset button. You have today.

Final Thought: Multiverse Mojo

What if every moment in your life is like standing at the edge of a cliff, and every choice you make is a leap?

Some leaps take you to soft landings. Some to wild rides. Some feel scary.But each one builds a universe.

Not just any universe. Your universe.

Knowing that, doesn't it make your next decision feel... epic?

So the next time you're facing a tough choice, remember:

You're not just picking a path—you're writing reality. So write it like a hero. Write it like an explorer. Write it like someone who knows that every choice can lead to adventure, growth, weirdness, and wonder.

Your decisions might feel small. But they echo across eternity. They shape new timelines. They birth new worlds.

You are the author of infinite stories. And you're living one of them right now.

At The End...

Congratulations, dear reader, for going through these 21 *"What Ifs"*

and daring to wander through wormholes of wonder, leap across galaxies of curiosity, and dive into oceans of imagination.

You've asked bold questions, played with impossible ideas, and explored worlds where science meets storytelling. Whether you paused time, vanished the moon, or chatted with aliens, you proved that curiosity has no limits—and neither does your mind.

But this is not the end.

This is just the beginning of your own "What If" journey.

So keep wondering.

Keep asking.

Keep imagining the impossible.

Because the future belongs to those who ask,
"What if...?"